To Trevor,

World War II Survival

The epic story of Leonid
Aleksandrov's journey from Russia
to Normandy and Berlin

Grant Williams

Raven Crest Books

ISBN-13: 978-0-9931909-1-9
ISBN-10: 0-99-319091-X

With thanks to my loving wife Sandy, who continued to run our family business whilst I spent so much time researching to bring this story to life.

FORWARD

This is the story of an ordinary man who had the most extraordinary life just because of his faith and circumstances. Born a Jew in Russia in 1917, Leon Aleksandrov spent his early years constantly moving around an increasingly anti-Semitic Europe until twenty-eight years later, finds himself sitting at Hitler's desk in the bombed out Reich Chancellery.

I was fortunate enough to be given sight of an extraordinary diary a few years ago. The story told was so moving, I felt compelled to write this book.

Because Leon was in such a famous regiment it was reasonably straight forward to piece together many of the missing components of his story. He had not left a great deal of detail about his advance through Europe after the D-Day landings, but there was ample detailed recorded history by the 8th Hussars archivists, to whom I am very grateful. By using this information, specifically from June 1944 – May 1945, I was able to construct a picture of his involvement in the advance through Europe. Having checked his military history as thoroughly as possible, we can be fairly certain that he was either there at the time of the events described or extremely close by.

In order to preserve the anonymity of his family, the names of all participants apart from the named historical figures have been changed.

This book should not be considered an academically accurate piece of work; it is an overview of an incredible time in European history and the effects on one man, told in his own words and expanded in mine. The family mentioned in the book are completely fictional and are used to allow the story to be told.

There have been so many books written about this period, it is my hope that this particular book sheds some light on the oft ignored period immediately after the end of the war.

FAMILY TREE

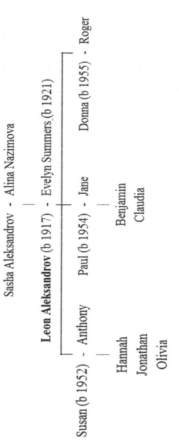

Sasha Aleksandrov - Alina Nazimova

Leon Aleksandrov (b 1917) - Evelyn Summers (b 1921)

Susan (b 1952) - Anthony   Paul (b 1954) - Jane   Donna (b 1955) - Roger

Hannah
Jonathan
Olivia

Benjamin
Claudia

CHAPTER 1

Christmas Eve, Finchley, North London 2001

Finchley was beautiful. There hadn't been much snow in December for many years, but it was looking increasingly likely there would be a white Christmas. Pavements, cars and walls were softened and the air was filled with heavy flakes. Footprints were already becoming shadows of themselves as the snow fell harder.

Rows of 1930s semi-detached houses lined the street which curved gently out of sight. Most of the trees planted along the pavements when the estate was built had been removed to allow for the two and three car families that now lived in Hawkedon Road. Many of the hedges that marked the boundaries of the houses had also been replaced by walls and gates, to improve security in the modern world and leave enough room for the four wheel drive. Children no longer played football in the road nor met to exchange jokes and stories. Personal interaction had changed but at Christmas, families would come together, if only for a day or two.

Many of the houses had been altered over the years with double glazing, extensions, cladding and porches. The uniformity of the pre-war construction was now an eclectic mix of individual improvements that made the street look scruffy and unloved, but with a dusting of snow the general outlines of the

1

houses remained the same. The table lamps that glowed inside had a warm and welcoming feel and none more so than number sixty-four.

Almost unchanged but perfectly kept, the house that stood on the south side, almost exactly equidistant from Albany Road and Sebastian Crescent, seemed smaller than the other houses around it. The original windows and front door with the stained glass inserts were an anachronism to the UPVC standard in the rest of the road. The house had a chocolate box look about it. It was still large by the building standards of the 1930s, with its four well-proportioned bedrooms and two large living rooms, but was now quite small compared to some of the enormous extensions others had undertaken.

A car pulled up in front and a middle-aged man jumped out of the driver's side and attempted to open the gates to the drive. They were stiff and had dropped over the years so that they had to be lifted as they were opened.

"Why didn't he ever change these gates? I don't even know why he kept them."

"I told you to just park in the road Roger, why do you even need to put the car in the drive? Nobody else has, I can see Anthony and Susan's car over there and Paul and Jane have parked over there," said Donna angrily.

It had been a dreadful journey up from Hampshire and Roger had been in a foul mood, as he always was when they came to visit Pepe. Pepe was Donna's father, Leon. She, and her brother and sister, had always known him as Pepe. He had once asked her elder sister Susan to call him Pepe as he had remembered this name from his time as a youngster

2

living in Europe. It had quickly caught on and everyone in the family had called him Pepe since she could remember.

Roger hated visiting Pepe. He didn't have time for the old man. Roger didn't have time for anybody; he was a man in a hurry, although nobody, especially Donna, quite knew where he was hurrying to. Donna thought he didn't like coming to Finchley because generally the rest of the family would be there and Roger, who thought himself superior to everybody else, actually felt inadequate. He would over compensate for this by being boorish and overbearing. Fortunately, the rest of the family had come to know Roger and accepted him for who he was, the husband of Donna whom they loved unconditionally.

"I don't want to leave it on the road, I only just collected it from the garage. On these roads anyone could slide into it, you know how long I had to wait to get this spec? People around here don't care, they would just slide into it and as likely as not drive off," Roger replied angrily.

The car crept to a halt right by the front door. Roger climbed out and closed the gates behind them. He lifted the boot lid and started taking the bags out.

"We could leave those until we have said hello to everyone, Roger," cursed Donna. "We are already hours late."

"Don't blame me! I had to close the deal. It was the biggest account I have got this year. It's not my fault your father lives four hours away, I never wanted to come in the first place. I don't want to have to come outside again on a night like this, you go in; I will only be a minute."

The door wasn't locked and the minute Donna

walked over the threshold, she could hear the familiar voices of her beloved family. She also knew how late they were and could smell the turkey in the oven and Pepe's favourite, the Borscht, on the hob. She was brought up along with her siblings on Borscht, a beetroot soup that Pepe himself had grown up with. He insisted on the traditional Ukrainian version with potatoes, beets, beet tops, cabbage and onions. Even though they had all left home years ago, they all met up at Pepe's at Christmas and Borscht was as important as presents and Father Christmas.

"Donna, is that you?" came the shrill from the kitchen. It was Jane.

They had always been close, but now the physical distance between them meant their meetings were even more excitable than usual.

Donna and Jane were very similar in appearance. Both shared a combination of looks from their parents. Their father had very pronounced cheekbones and a pointed nose. They both had these but in a very feminine way, which made them both quite beautiful and they had their mother Evelyn's curly dark hair. Individually, they were very attractive but together they were very striking… and loud.

The meeting of the sisters drove the already intense decibel level up a notch or two. The house was already full of noise. The radio was on, entertaining the teenage grandchildren, who were having their own animated debate over the virtues of Jay Z. The five grandchildren, ranging from fifteen to nineteen, had grown up very close. They lived only a few miles apart in another area of north London and had spent many holidays together. Donna and Jane's brother, Anthony, was deep in conversation with

Jane's husband, Paul, over the title race between Man United, Chelsea and Arsenal. They were both season ticket holders but for the two different London Clubs. It was a healthy rivalry.

"God, I need a drink," said Roger as he crashed through the doors with two large bags.

"Evening Rog," shouted Paul and Anthony in unison. Jane broke away from hugging her sister to give Roger a big kiss on the lips.

"How's my favourite brother-in-law, still so handsome," she said.

"Cut the BS, I am your only brother-in-law. Hello Jane, lovely to see you too," replied Roger.

"Your wine is here," shouted Hannah from the kitchen.

"Lovely to see you Uncle Roger." Hannah walked through from the kitchen, holding a glass of Shiraz. Eighteen years old and in her first year at university, Hannah was a chip off the old block. As beautiful as her mother, she had her Dad Anthony's height and dark looks, but all the calming attributes of her mother, Susan. There was something so personable about Hannah, everyone loved her.

"Lovely to see you, Hannah," he said as he leant forward to greet her.

"I will take those for you, Roger," said Jonathan, Hannah's elder brother by a year. Slightly taller than Hannah with the same family looks, a fine looking young man. Jonathan was not academically inclined and now worked in his father's successful distribution business. Jonathan grabbed the bags and made light work of them as he sprinted up the stairs.

Roger and Donna walked through into the lounge. It was a picture of Suburban Christmas, but from a bygone age. The fire was roaring, Christmas cards were everywhere, with a lovely tree in the corner with the old fashioned multi-coloured lights flickering. These would have been the original lights that Pepe put on the first tree he ever bought when the children were growing up. As an electrical engineer, he had been able to keep them going all these years, meticulously packing them away every time. Also on the tree were small candle holders to light the traditional candles as they did after every Christmas Eve Dinner. In traditional fashion, Pepe had knocked the two large lounges as a through lounge. This was very popular in the 1950s and Pepe's one structural alteration he made to the original fabric of the house.

In front of the fire, Benjamin, Claudia and Olivia were chatting together. Benjamin and Claudia were the children of Jane and Paul, seventeen and fifteen respectively, while Olivia was the youngest of Anthony and Susan's children at seventeen. Seeing the three of them together in front of the fire brought a lump to Donna's throat. She and Roger had never had children. They had had some problems initially and Roger didn't want to pursue anything through the doctor and would never consider adoption. He said that if it was going to happen then it would. Although they continued to try, Donna knew that Roger wasn't that bothered, he had his career, but she had an empty heart and as she saw her nieces and nephews grow, she felt the life ebb away from her. She spent as much time as she could with them but when they had to move away with Roger's work, she lost her faith.

Hannah and Jonathan brought through a tray of champagne glasses that had already been poured and passed them round. The family picture was perfect and complete. As they raised their glasses, they turned to the man sat quietly in the chair next to the fire and toasted:

"To Pepe, Happy Christmas."

Leon Aleksandrov was in his eighty-fourth year. He looked younger than his years; he was grey, but still had a good head of hair. Although he was sat in his chair, you could tell that he was tall and had been a strong man. He had a small grey beard but his eyes were burning as bright as ever.

"*L'Chaim*," shouted Pepe.

"To Life," shouted everyone in unison.

"*Budmo*," shouted Pepe.

"Health and Happiness."

This had been the routine on Christmas Eve at sixty-four Hawkedon Road, Finchley for as long as anyone could remember. *L'Chaim* was the Yiddish toast and *Budmo* the Ukrainian, representing the two backgrounds to the family's life. Only two things had changed. Firstly, everyone had grown up, even the grandchildren now had a glass of champagne. Secondly, Evelyn was not with them. Evelyn had been the love of Leon's life. Married during the war, they had been together for almost sixty years. Evelyn had passed away two years ago; this was the second Christmas without her. She had been the matriarch of the family, the life and soul. No more colourful character would you ever meet. Leon brought the Jewish thread to the family but Evelyn was Church of England so the family celebrated Christmas and had been brought up in that tradition.

"To Evie," said Olivia.

There was a pause and then collectively, but a little more subdued, everyone chinked and repeated the phrase. Evie was the name that everyone used, their grandmother had never been happy with her name, which was very popular when she was born, she always insisted on the abbreviation.

Seeing the moment needed some uplifting, Susan asked for some help and the room changed as some of the girls moved to the kitchen to finish off the preparations for dinner. Benjamin, Claudia and Olivia all sat with their grandfather. He had cried a little at the thought of his darling Evie. They had been closer than most couples. They had stayed together all those years in the same house they had bought a few years after the war. They had brought up three wonderful children together and had spent so much time with all of their grandchildren who lived close by. As soon as Leon had retired from work, they spent as much time as possible with their family, attending every event for their grandchildren no matter how small. It had been such a wrench when Donna had moved away, but they would travel to Hampshire to visit her as often as possible. Leon knew that he had lived a charmed life. He began to cry again. Tears welled up in his eyes and began to run down his cheek.

"Pepe, are you alright?" asked Claudia.

"I am fine, Claudy, I was just thinking of your grandmother and the time we spent together with you in the park and it made me very happy, that was all."

"Is there anything I can get you?" she asked

"I am a little hot here by the fire, could you help me through to the other room please? I would like a little rest before dinner," replied Leon.

Claudia helped Pepe to his feet but, despite his years, he didn't really need any help, he just liked the grandchildren to think they could be of assistance.

Pepe was still very independent. He had not abused his body through his long life. He had seen too much in his earlier years and knew how precious it was, that it was a gift from God. He had savoured every minute of his life.

Claudia helped Pepe through to the other room. As they walked through, he turned to those left to say that he was fine, not to worry, that he was just going to rest and repeated the same message as he passed the serving hatch that linked the kitchen to the lounge. His daughters smiled to him as he went by.

Claudia supported Pepe as he lowered himself into his favourite chair by the window and put a blanket across his knees. Although the heating was on, it was much cooler away from the fire. Leon looked out of the window into the middle distance.

"Are you ok, Grandpapa, can I get you anything?" asked Claudia.

"Why did you call me Grandpapa?" asked Leon.

"I don't know, I wasn't really thinking, do you mind?" she replied.

"Of course not, I am your Grandpapa. Do you know why everyone calls me Pepe?" he said.

"Not really, it is just something I grew up with, I have always known you as Pepe, I don't know why I called you Grandpapa really, I suppose it was because we visited my father's family yesterday and I always call Grandpa Michael, Grandpapa," said Claudia.

"Would you like to know where Pepe comes from? It is a story from a long time ago, I am not sure you will find it very interesting, but if you want to indulge an old man?" said Leon.

Claudia loved her grandfather but wasn't sure she wanted to sit and endure some old story. He had never really told stories before. Leon had always been the quiet one, it was Grandma Evie who was always talking; stories, songs, she was so lively and always entertained the family. Claudia really wanted to get away and join her cousins, who were always really good fun, but she knew a few minutes with her grandpa wouldn't kill her.

"Of course, Pepe," she replied.

CHAPTER 2

June 13ᵗʰ 1917 Kiev in the Ukraine

"It all started a long time ago, too long for you to imagine, in 1917. I was born on June thirteenth, actually it was June twenty-sixth according to the English Julian calendar. I was born in Uman in the district of Kiev which was then Russian Ukraine. That is why we always toast '*Budmo*' because it is Ukrainian for Health and Happiness. My grandparents, your great grandparents, were practising Jews, while my father, Sasha, and mother, Alina, were less observant.

We left Russia during the Revolution of 1920. It is hard for you to imagine, living here in England where everything is safe and secure, that life could be anything else. My father was a craftsman and had his own business, which meant he had double the trouble. He was Jewish and others thought he was wealthy. The Jews were hated, I don't understand why, we worked hard and created employment, but for centuries we had been regarded as outsiders, but at least tolerated.

Everyone reads in history books about 1917 and the removal of the Tsar. Everyone thinks they were replaced by the Bolsheviks but that came a year later. The Tsar couldn't fight the revolution because the army was so weak fighting Germany in the west, you see there was a terrible war going on at the time, the First World War. Russia was bankrupt fighting a war

11

we couldn't win or afford. The Bolsheviks took over, sued for peace with the Germans and then fought amongst themselves, you may have heard of the fight between the Red Bolsheviks and the White Anti-Bolsheviks? Maybe you saw Dr Shivago with Omar Sharif? The Red Bolsheviks eventually won and there was a redistribution of land from the rich to the poor. In the meantime, they murdered the Royal family, the Romanovs, even their dog, can you imagine it? They say the Royal family were all lined up and were shot one by one, could you imagine that happening today? The Queen, Prince Phillip, the Corgis? Ordinary Russians were in shock. Terrible things were done during the revolution, whole villages were destroyed but it was still such a shock when we heard about the Romanovs, we knew then that no-one was safe.

The Ukraine had declared independence during this time using their Government, The Rada. They enlisted the help of the Jewish community to combat Poland, who saw an opportunity to take over parts of the Ukraine, but this harmony was short lived.

There was anti-Semitism, and what they called The Pogroms, destroying all things Jewish. 100,000 Jews died from 1919 – 1920 fighting the Polish and another 100,000 were murdered by the Ukrainian authorities or the counter revolutionary Russian army units. Everyone remembers the Holocaust but 100,000 Jews were murdered, men, women and children, and this is never spoken about. That is why we always toast *L'Chaim*.

In 1920, the Bolsheviks took over the Ukraine and the persecution got worse. We had to leave and so did 300,000 others. We had to leave because of our faith, there was no other reason, it had been like this since the Romans. When the Romans took over Jerusalem seventy years after the death of Christ, they killed a million Jews. Here in England, in 1290, King Edward banished all Jews from the country. It has always happened. People always talk about how hard the Jews have been on the Palestinians, but we have had to fight to save our race all of our history. We do not want it to be like that, we never have, we have always been hunted, it has always been that way.

I was three years old. We secretly crossed the River Dniestre in a rowing boat at night. I travelled with my grandmother travelling separately to my mother and father, as it might be safer. There were hundreds of us paying to get a ride in a boat. I remember clutching the blanket my mother had knitted for me. I didn't understand what was happening. It seemed like an adventure, that's what my grandmother told me, until the food ran out and I was hungry. All I remember after that was travelling and being hungry.

We crossed the river into Romania. All Ukrainian Jews had been granted citizenship there after the First World War. This place was known as Bessarabia, now it is known as Moldova. We made the journey to the capital Kishenew where we met up with my father; we stayed there with friends and family, constantly moving house for ten months.

In Romania, we were persecuted as Jews again. My father was unable to start a business and make a life, so we left. My Grandmother wanted to stay and lived with my Uncle and Aunt in Galatz on the Danube. The three of us travelled to Warsaw, the Polish capital. Once again, we packed our things into a few suitcases and made the journey. I thought that life was all about travelling, as I had not known a home. We only stayed in Warsaw a short time before we travelled to Danzig on the Baltic, which was then a free city, situated between Germany and Poland. It had been created at the end of the First World War as a kind of buffer between Germany and Poland. It was like a lost city without a country, an ideal place for the Jews to go to. I don't really know why we ended up there. I think this was a staging post for migrration to the United States or Canada but in 1924 the Johnson Act stopped all Jewish immigration into those two countries. Nobody wanted us.

I can only assume my father found work because I started school as an infant and Junior. I was taught in German from five to eight years. I was at school with lots of Jews. History says there were 136,000 of us in Danzig, which was Gdansk in Polish. I remember this as a good time. We lived in more or less one home and I made friends and knew where I was going every day. I loved the routine and had some toys. I know it seems strange to hear that a five year old should be happy with routine, but until then I never knew what I was doing from one day to the next and I had no roots. I think that things improved for us in Danzig, I remember we used to go for walks and my mother would buy me ice-cream. I was very happy.

In 1925, I presume because we knew we couldn't go to the United States, we moved to Krakow in southern Poland, where I had to speak Polish. I eventually went to a Polish Gymnasium which was a grammar school where I had to pass an entrance exam for all the subjects in Polish. I was only eight years old but knew that if I didn't learn the language, I couldn't go to school. I quickly learnt as school was so much better than the boredom of being at home. I was the only Jew in my class and the atmosphere was very anti-Semitic. Some of the bigger boys picked on me and called me all sorts of names for being Jewish, the teachers didn't stop them but I quickly became thick skinned about it. My parents made friends with other Jewish families so their children became my friends. We never talked about how horrible the others were to us though.

It seemed like trouble just followed us around. Almost as soon as we had arrived in Poland it went from being a democracy to Authoritarian rule and with it came riots against Jews. Sometimes I wondered if there were some Jews somewhere who had been horrible people and done terrible things to cause everyone to hate us but my father told me that it was the way it was, that we were hated because God loved us so much and everyone else was jealous.

We couldn't stay and sought refuge by moving somewhere with more liberal attitudes. By now I had lived in four countries in six years, so hoped we would settle down somewhere peaceful where I could really get on with my studies and make friends.

We moved to Berlin in 1928, the capital of Germany."

CHAPTER 3

Berlin 1928, into the Hornet's nest

"As an eleven year old whose life had been constantly on the move, Berlin was so exciting. Berlin in 1928 was decadent and bourgeois. This was the Weimar era, the time of Leni Riefenstahl, Anna May Wong, Marlene Dietriech and the Kit Kat Club. I was only eleven and although I didn't really know of these things, Berlin flourished culturally, and became an important metropolis with film, theatre, cabaret and thousands of bars and restaurants. We had been constantly on the move for six years, but at last we were in a liberal City full of excitement and opportunity, where perhaps being Jewish wouldn't be held against us.

My father found some work and we settled into an apartment in the Jewish district of Mitte. We lived in a road off the main Oranienburger Strasse in a good sized flat above a bagel shop. The smell of freshly baked bagels used to waft up through the boards every morning and I would run down to get them fresh and warm for breakfast. I had a room of my own and thought life couldn't get any better than this. We were very close to the Tiergarden where I would often play with my mother and father.

Not for the first time, I had to relearn all of my schoolwork, this time in German. I was accepted into the Werner Siemens Gymnasium, I started in the second year aged eleven. The school had been founded by the inventor and carried his name. The emphasis was on exercise, which suited me; I loved the outdoor life. I was good at sport and my fellow pupils accepted me, I was popular and being Jewish didn't seem to be a problem for the first time in my life. I was very happy but I know things were quite hard for my parents. These were difficult times in Germany and from what my parents said, in other parts of the world too. In 1929 was something called the Great Crash which happened in America. Papa said that perhaps it was a good thing we didn't get on the boat after all.

Wall Street had its effect on Germany and on our lives. Within a year, the German economy was in ruins. Nobody wanted to buy our exports and the loans we were used to from America disappeared. Suddenly there were queues for soup and bread along the streets. My mother's warming stews no longer had meat, just broth and some vegetables. Almost overnight, the living standards of so many Berliners, and I assume all Germans, were ruined.

The atmosphere started to change. Gone were the happy times, everyone was hungry and looking for a solution. Suddenly, the people of Berlin envied the farmers with their plentiful supply of food and the talk changed to politics. I was only thirteen, but could see what was happening.

In 1932 we had some joy in our house when my mother gave birth to a baby girl, a sister for me. She was called Anna. That same year, I had my Bar Mitzvah. My real name, that none of you know, was Leonid Aleksandrov, but my father, gave me the familiar name of Pepe. This was a form of the name

Joseph and meant 'God will add'. That is why I like to be called Pepe, so now you know!"

***

"Wow," said Claudia, who had been immersed in her grandfather's every word despite her first concerns. "Why were you not always called Pepe?"

"This was a familiar name that only my mother and father called me, it is something that is only used by the family, which is why I like you all to call me Pepe, it reminds me I have family." The old man smiled at his grand-daughter. Claudia had just been sat kneeling, expecting to get away after a few minutes but she was absorbed in his story and repositioned herself with some cushions to get more comfortable. Benjamin, who had overhead his grandfather talking about the Red and White Bolsheviks, had also joined them. He was studying the Russian Revolution at School for A Levels and recognized the names. He sat on a footstool that had been beautifully covered by his grandmother years earlier.

"Go on, Pepe," said Benjamin. "What happened next?"

Leon shuffled in his chair and Claudia leant forwards to adjust his blanket that had slipped slightly.

"We were very happy again for a while but things were clearly changing. In 1933, the student union in Germany proclaimed a nationwide 'Action against the Un-German Spirit' and books were burned in the street," said Leon.

"What, all the books?" asked Claudia.

"No, not all the books, but the list was pretty long,

it was mainly about anything that wasn't considered pure German and especially about the German *Volk*. After the burnings, a whole list of books were then banned and it was very dangerous to be caught with any of them, especially if you were a Jew. They banned books on Communism, Pacifism, sexuality, but most critically anything by Jewish authors. A hundred years before a Jewish German Poet called Heinrich Heine had said, 'Where they burn books, one day they will burn people'. Very prosaic, don't you think? Funnily enough, he was banned by the German authorities even then.

In 1935 at the age of only forty-seven, my father died. He was by now running a business with his brother, Saul. They were traders, specializing in leather. He had been on a train on a business visit when he had a heart attack. He was very young, perhaps it was the strain of the constant movement, perhaps it was the persecution, I don't know, but as you can see, weak hearts are not necessarily hereditary!" Leon banged on his chest with his fist. They all laughed together.

"He was buried at the Weissensee Cemetery in Berlin. At the age of only eighteen, I was the head of the family and felt like I had the burden of the world on my shoulders. That is more or less the same age as you are now Benjamin, imagine being the head of the family and responsible for everything."

Leon continued. "I had seen father become more depressed in the time leading up to his death. He had seen the rise of Hitler and the Nazi Party. Hitler had come to power in 1933 and Papa had said that life might get difficult for us again because we were Jews. He talked of Hitler´s book, *Mein Kampf*. He had read it and feared what it said, although he never told us. I never read the book; I was more interested in sport and girls at that time. I have read it since and it was pretty clear what Hitler intended if he ever got absolute power, which he did. I sometimes wonder if the allied leaders had ever bothered to read it, I am sure the extermination of the Jews wouldn't have come as such a shock if they had; it had all been laid out in Hitler's book.

I continued with my studies and school life continued more or less normally. The Werner Siemens Gymnasium was the only school in Berlin, apart from the Karl Marx School, that operated a 'Pupils' Parliament' entirely represented by the boys and chaired and administrated by pupils, the teachers attending as observers only. It didn't seem strange at the time because that was how things were, but the Nazi boys started to come to school in Hitler Youth Uniforms, representing the Nazi Party, while the majority of the delegates were members of the Social Democratic, Communist Liberal and Centre parties. We were quite envious of the Nazi boys with their smart uniforms and the fact that they 'belonged' and had something to believe in. At that time, the Nazi Party was the great hope, you have to remember the economy was bankrupt and things were very bad for many people.

Because of the problems in the country, debates and discussions became more controversial and often very heated, but I never felt threatened, we were all school chums living together and it was stimulating.

Gradually, the repressive policies of the government caused the school to be closed down in 1935. The reason stated by the authorities was that the school was overrun by adherents of left wing views and too many Jews – expressed by the German term '*Verjudet*'. The well-tempered political discussions had degenerated into blaming the Jews for everything in line with the Government policies. Most of my German friends had sided with this. It was difficult for them not to. By then, the Hitler Youth were being used by the Brownshirts, who were Hitler´s private police force, to spy on everyone and report if anyone was helping the Jews. Everyone was in a very difficult situation."

"Tea anyone?" called Donna. "Pepe? Claudia? Benjamin? What are you three talking about?"

Leon looked across to Donna and raised his forefinger indicating he would like a cup.

"Tea for me too," said Claudia, "no sugar though, I am dieting."

"Hot chocolate for me," said Benjamin.

"What are you all talking about? You seem deep in discussion," said Donna.

"Pepe is telling us about his time in Germany, it is really interesting, we have been doing this in school for A Levels. Olivia, you should come and listen to Grandpa, you are doing Politics for A Level," said Benjamin.

"Why not, are you coming, Hannah?" said Olivia.

It wasn't really Hannah's thing, but her best friend had just lost her grandfather so she felt some guilt at not spending enough time with her own Pepe. The four of them formed an arc around their Grandfather, Benjamin on the footstool, the other three sat on assorted cushions. The drinks weren't long in arriving.

"Grandpapa has been telling me how they had to

leave Russia and escape in a boat across the river and how he lived all over Europe. He has just got to the bit where he is in Berlin and the Nazis have taken power, it's really exciting," said Claudia.

Leon took a few sips of his drink and passed the cup and saucer back to Claudia. Everyone else had a mug, but Leon was used to a cup and saucer, it was something that Evie had insisted on all their married life and he wasn't about to change now. He had really liked that Evie insisted on it because his mother had as well. He remembered on many occasions the fine china being carefully unpacked and packed again every time they had to move.

He continued, drifting back into his story, Claudia could already tell in his own mind he was back there, part of the buildings, part of Berlin.

"I was now eighteen and because of the school closure I had to stop further education. In September of 1935, the Nuremberg Laws were passed making all Jews second class citizens. We were not allowed to hoist the Reich Flag but were encouraged to display the Jewish Colours. At first, we didn't mind, the Jews had been persecuted for hundreds of years, these were just flags, we had been through worse. We were banned from joining the Army. known as the Wehrmacht. This didn't bother us, the military was never a profession for Jews anyway, but later that year the Law for the Protection of German Blood and Honor was passed, preventing marriage between Jews and non-Jews. This was a disaster, there were so many pretty German girls!" He laughed and so did his little audience.

More laws were passed and very soon, Jews, half

Jews, even quarter Jews, were no longer citizens of Germany. In 1936, we were banned from all professional jobs so we could not exert any influence in education, politics and industry. I was lucky, I joined my father's partner, my Uncle Saul, in his leather business. This occupation was not what I had hoped for, but these were difficult times and I was pleased to have a job at all. It gave me freedom and income and I was able to learn to drive, passing my test at eighteen. I was the only person able to drive the motor which was attached to the business. This enabled me to increase my ability to attract the interest of the fairer sex, together with my mate, Isaak Kanchinsky."

"Were girls all you thought about, Pepe?" asked Benjamin.

"Hah! Are girls all you think about, Benjamin? I thought so, remember I was much the same age as you are now, working, driving and chasing girls!

Isaak and I would drive all over Berlin in the company van. We thought we were something very special, and I suppose we were. There weren't many lads our age that had a vehicle and it helped with the girls. Of course, as the political climate was changing and the relationship between the Germans and the Jews was changing too, some people looked at us in a funny way."

"Is Isaak the same as Great Uncle Isaak?" asked Claudia.

"Yes, that's right," said Leon. "He has been a close family friend for as long as I can remember, he and I have been through a lot together.

Amongst our friends there remained a few Aryan German boys, who, although they were forced to join the Hitler Youth, never agreed with the Nazi regime. This was borne out by the fact that two of those boys I was to meet again in 1985 and 1993 and I know that they remained anti-Nazi. It was very difficult for them, they had grown up with us Jewish boys, but everywhere they were being told not to mix with us; by the authorities, by their own parents, people were becoming fearful as stories spread of intellectuals being arrested. The atmosphere was getting unpleasant. Often people had to appear to hate the Jews just to avoid being arrested, everyone was spying on everyone else, there really was a terrible sense of fear.

As a foreign subject, I was still a Romanian national; I had a certain amount of freedom of movement and could travel abroad. In some ways, I was glad I was not German, it would have made things much harder for me being Jewish. Did you know that in 1933 there were 522,000 Jews living in Germany but by 1939 there were only 214,000! Many fled abroad but many were arrested, imprisoned or murdered. People just disappeared. That was the most frightening thing.

In our little apartment block, a lovely lady, Mrs Edelman, lived on the top floor. She was in her fifties and was married to a jeweller called Schim. They had moved to our apartment block the year before. They did not show their wealth but we could tell that they had a lot of money. I wondered why they had moved to our apartment block. They had owned a very expensive villa in one of the best districts in Berlin but were now in a modest, two bedroom apartment. I later found out that they had been forced to sell their jewelry business to a German competitor very quickly at a knock down price and then their house. They had moved here but within a few months Schim Edelman had been taken away by the *Schutzstaffel*, which were like the Police Force, known as the Protection Squadrons, you might know them as the *SS*. He was sent to the Columbia Haus facility in Berlin, a big prison where political prisoners were kept. We didn't know why he had been arrested. It later turned out that he had been trying to get his property back through the German courts. The authorities didn't like this and arrested him.

His wife tried to visit him every day but each time she went, the cost of the bribes to see him went up and up. Eventually, she had no money left. He was then transferred to Dachau concentration camp. We never heard from him again. My mother would go up to see Mrs Edelman, but after a few weeks she would not even answer her door. We would sometimes see her go out late at night to buy some food, shuffling past in her old coat with her yellow star of David on her sleeve. You see, by this time, as Jews we all had to wear the star of David."

"What happened to Mrs Edelman?" asked Hannah.

"I don't know for sure, I had to leave Berlin and never saw her again. Her fate was the same as many others. It was always hardest on the older people," said Pepe, looking down at his blanket.

"I don't understand how the Germans could just make him sell his business. What about the law? Nobody could make you sell your business and your house here in England, why didn't the police stop it, it couldn't have been right," said Claudia.

"Oh, lovely Claudia, how innocent you are,"

replied Pepe.

"It was the police and the authorities that made them sell their business. I know it is difficult to understand, but within a few years, Jews went from being successful business people who created wealth and employed people to being regarded as vermin, taking away German jobs and making people poor. The Jews were blamed for everything. The Nazi party had very good propaganda and owned the police. Everyone was afraid. Every day, at every opportunity, the German people were told that the Jews were to blame and eventually through fear and being continually told so, they believed it. We lost all our rights and within a couple of years we had none at all. What happened to the Edelmans eventually happened to every Jew in Berlin, then Germany and then in every country that Germany invaded. In *Mein Kampf,* Hitler had talked about the power of lies. He had said that the Jews were great liars and that if you told a big enough lie, everyone would believe it. The Nazis, in fact, did this, their lies became bigger and bigger, until they were believable, I often wondered how the Nazis felt about doing exactly the same as what they blamed the Jews for."

Pepe took a breath. They could all tell that he was wrenching inside. Even though he appeared calm and collected, the journey he was taking was bringing back all the memories.

"As I said, because I could travel, I visited my grandmother in Romania and an aunt and uncle in Warsaw quite frequently. Being a foreign subject in Germany, the gradually increasing government repression did not affect me physically. I could, in the company of other Russian *émigrés*, continue a reasonably active social life, albeit that we were not able, as Jews, to employ German domestic staff or German labour in the business, but this did not bother us, we were able to find enough Jews in the community to work for us. We were also unable to visit theatres, concerts and other entertainments unless they were organized and performed by Jewish artists, but by this time the arts were generally being restricted by the Nazis and freedom of speech and expression was restricted, it was ok if you enjoyed Wagner! The Nazis loved Wagner! Can you imagine now not being allowed to go to the cinema because you are Jewish! How did it all happen?"

"Was there nothing you could do?" asked Susan, who had come across with a plate of Florentines, a particular favourite of Pepe's. She sat on the edge of the sofa next to Jonathan, who had just come to see why everyone was sat around his grandfather. Susan craned in to hear him speak. She had never heard him mention the war before. It was as though his only life was the one she knew in suburban Finchley, her kind father who worked hard and provided for them, who led a quiet life with his loving family. Pepe took a Florentine and savoured it as he ate.

"I know it seems hard to believe today, that we should have been restricted to all of these things, but in those days it just happened, every day there was a new law and every day the German people became more frightened of the Nazis and had to join them," said Leon.

"Aren't you angry?" asked Olivia. "Your neighbours and friends turning on you?"

"They didn't have much choice. They were ordinary people and every day they were being told

28

that it was the Jews who were responsible for the Depression, the unemployment, the lack of food, that the Jews had all the money. It was relentless. The Nazis offered hope. At that time, people weren't being murdered, we were just the scapegoats. Lots of people did not agree but were becoming frightened because the police were everywhere. I cannot blame them," said Leon. "The newspapers were controlled by the Nazis, it was unavoidable."

"What would you have done, Pepe if it had been the other way round?" asked Benjamin.

"I asked myself the same question thousands of times in the past. I don't know. It is very difficult, unless you were there at the time. I would like to think I might have stood up and said something, but even today we don't. Were all the Jews bad? No, of course not, people were just afraid. Let me tell you, at that time, I was seeing a lovely Jewish girl called Mady. She worked in a little patisserie, so not only was she very pretty but every time we went out, she would bring a little boxed, beautifully wrapped, with ribbons and always a little treat, strudel, chocolate cake, it was heaven. She had the loveliest legs and always wore light floaty dresses to show them off. Susan, my sweet, pass me my little satchel on the cupboard there, please."

Susan stretched up and brought down a worn brown leather satchel, like a small school bag, and passed it to Pepe. He opened the buckle and after looking through a sheath of papers, pulled out a worn photograph. It was in black and white and a small corner was missing. He held the photo up for all to see.

"Can you see the sign? 'This bench is for Jews

only'. Can you imagine it, walking through an open park on a summer's day but we can only sit on a bench marked for the Jews! I am sorry about the photo, Isaak took it to get the sign, I wish he had taken one of Mady's legs! It is funny though, at the time, we didn't think too much about it, we were young and just trying to enjoy ourselves and things weren't too bad, at least the shops were full of food now. Some things were better under the Nazis.

Hitler did everything he could to appease the International Community. Countries were always talking about embargoes and diplomacy, but nothing much happened. In 1936, the Nazis had held the Olympics in Berlin. It was a show of strength, not one of aggression and everything was designed to show the Germans as a peace loving nation. I went to the Olympics and watched Jesse Owen win the sprint. It was such a great event and something I will never forget. The Nazis could really lay on a spectacle. The flags and torches were quite incredible. In 1936, they didn't have the reputation that we all know them for now. The crowd went wild when Jesse Owens won the 100m but Hitler wasn't there to give him his medal. We all knew why, the Nazis had the same view of black people, as a race inferior to the Aryans, the fact that a black man raced past Aryans would have been humiliating for Hitler.

I was able to go on holiday to Czechoslovakia and Hungary until 1937, when I decided I could no longer remain in Germany for political reasons. I was now twenty. Under new laws, Jews were being penalized financially for being Jewish. I realized I would just be working harder and harder to pay for the Nazis. I had seen first-hand what had happened to the Edelmans and I knew that the Nazis would have their eyes on our leather business. I then realised that one of the reasons there was now food in the shops after years of deprivation because of the Great Depression was that all the Jews' wealth was being taken and redistributed to the German people. In June, a young Jew by the name of Helmut Hirsch was executed for being in a plot to kill the Nazi Leadership, including Hitler. I had been sitting in a café not far from home when my friend Olga came running up to tell me. She was crying because she knew what it meant for the rest of us. This gave the Nazis the excuses they needed. The next year saw *Kristallnacht*, when all hell broke loose, shops were smashed and synagogues set alight. 30,000 Jewish men were arrested. I got out just in time. As a Jewish man of twenty years, I would certainly have been arrested and ended up in a work camp."

CHAPTER 4

Imprisoned in France

"I left Berlin aged twenty, leaving my mother and sister with the intention of meeting up somewhere at some time. I headed for Switzerland, where I stayed in Lausanne for about six months.

Here, I studied French, taught a little German and Russian, and whiled away the days walking around Lake Geneva and into the hillside. I spent time in the Old Quarter, La Cité, visiting the medieval cathedral. Because it is a university city and has many parks and outdoors spaces, I quickly made friends and enjoyed myself there, but knew I couldn't stay. At the end of that year, I moved on to Paris on a fourteen day transit visa. There, I met up once again with my childhood and school friend, Isaak, who had arrived in Paris via Italy, having left Berlin at the same time and for the same reasons. It was just as though we had never been apart. This was one of the most exciting times of my life. We were twenty-one years old and living in Paris. We didn't have any family with us and were completely free, having escaped the Nazi regime. We felt that life was looking up for us.

In Paris, we shared a room in a dingy hotel in the Latin Quarter called Grand Hôtel de Suez. We just managed to get by on £6 per month each, occasionally augmenting our very meagre capital by giving English lessons, although our own expertise was limited to our German school English. It meant we were able to visit some of the fine houses in Paris and sometimes get a meal. We were poor but very happy and very free. We quickly found the cheap bars and found the girls of Paris every bit as pretty as the girls in Berlin. Our days were spent walking along the boulevards, drinking coffee in the day when we weren't teaching, and stretching out a carafe of wine at night in the risqué bars around Montmartre with the artisans and the working girls.

As my resident's permit allowed me to stay only fourteen days in France, I experienced continuous problems with the police, spending days in the Prefectures Head Office, appealing for extensions, until in May 1939, they refused any further prolongation and gave me seven days to leave the country. It was impossible for me to leave France as I had no entry visa to anywhere else. Freedom of movement was being restricted all over Europe at this time. I sought the help of a Socialist member of the French Parliament, whom I had met on a previous occasion. Whilst he was unable to help me get the expulsion order rescinded, he suggested that I should leave Paris and go to Nevers, which was his constituency. It later became the demarcation line between Vichy and occupied France.

He felt that as long as I registered with the local police there, they would not trouble me and I could stay there until some other way could be found to leave France and enter another country legally. The journey to the Loire in Burgundy was a hundred and fifty miles through beautiful countryside. I had a feeling of optimism in the fresh air as the sun shone in through the windows of the train as it made its way into the heart of France. I remember that I had packed some cheese and bread and a half bottle of wine. Although I did not know what to expect, there was a feeling of tranquillity.

I arrived at Nevers late in the afternoon and found some lodgings at a cheap hotel. I had no work and little money and didn't know a soul in this small French town. At least it gave me a chance to practice the French I had learnt in Lausanne, although the sophisticated tongue of the Swiss was a far cry from the earthy language of this small town. I felt like the outsider I had always been as the locals wanted little to do with me, especially when they found out I had come from Paris. At that time, the country folk were wary of the Parisians, wary of everyone in fact, as the refugees from the Spanish civil war were constantly passing through.

The scheme devised for me by my Socialist Parliamentarian seemed to work for a little while, but in 1939 Nevers was only a small town. The appearance of an obvious stranger strolling around would eventually attract the attention of the authorities at a very sensitive time. A climax was reached when my friend Isaak, much to my delight, came to visit me. So now there were two of us wandering around the streets and we did not look like the typical French farmer. We stayed in the same room in the Hôtel Terminus, which was ideally situated – opposite the police station! Like the Hôtel de Suez, the Hôtel Terminus was, at best, basic but we had little money and little choice.

On the 22nd of May Hitler had signed the Pact of Steel with Mussolini. Everyone knew war was coming whatever the politicians said. Hitler had already threatened the Jews in a speech in January and the mood was turning.

For a birthday celebration, Isaak had bought some baguettes and sausages for a birthday snack. There was a knock at the door.

Two men, in trench coats with boots, introduced themselves as officers of the *Sûrete Nationalé,* not the local police, wanting to know what we were doing in Nevers and what our business was. They were very official and very abrupt."

"Wasn't this all a bit severe, Grandpa?" asked Benjamin.

"You have to understand what was happening at the time. France had been inundated with refugees after the Spanish Civil war, which had just ended. The French Government wanted to use all of this labour to build huge projects in France and to put some of the experienced fighters into the French Army to fight the Nazis, should war come, but there was an atmosphere of anti-communism and anti-Jew hysteria. The leader of the government was a man called Daladier and he ordered the mass internment of immigrants from 'Greater Germany'. Rather than using all of these people who hated the Nazis, the French wanted to get rid of them. So here we were, in front of these two guys sort of like the Secret Police. They arrested us both and handed us over to the local police. The charge was suspicion of infringing national security. Isaak still had a valid permit, although it was for Paris, and he was released. I received an expulsion order from France and was therefore detained in a police cell until the morning when I was transferred to the local prison known as the *Maison d'Arrêt.* You didn´t know that your

Grandfather had been to prison, did you? I wish I could say it was for some grand event, unfortunately it was just because I did not have the right papers.

My friend did not abandon me though, and later that day Isaak visited me in jail. It was a very strange experience, both being kept apart in something like a Catholic confessional kiosk, with a warder standing between our dividing grille. Isaak had brought me some food but the guard took it and never gave it to me. Isaak then returned to Paris. I wondered if I would ever see my friend again. I was very frightened.

The jail was damp and very cold and I told myself that I would never complain again about the Hotel de Suez, which suddenly seemed like a five star hotel in comparison.

A few days later, the Investigating Judge – the *'Juge d'Instruction'* , ordered me to come to the *Palais de Justice* for an interview to establish on what charge to prosecute me. I was taken from the jail to the *Palais de Justice* through the streets and parks of Nevers, manacled to a prison officer and with other as yet un-sentenced criminals, with me in my usual smart garb. I was terrified.

Whilst living in Berlin, intellectuals and prominent Jews started disappearing. Nobody knew why exactly and there were rumours of treason and crimes against the state, but we all knew it was the purge against the Jews. Because of the Edelmans I knew a little bit about the concentration camps and I knew that a Jew could end up there for no particular reason. In the last few months, the French newspapers were full of anti-Semitic articles and it was clear that this was not just a German issue. I wondered if I would end up in one of the camps. It crossed my mind that I might just be taken out and shot to save on the paperwork.

Eventually, there was a court case in which I had to defend myself. I was offered a lawyer but could not afford one. I thought if they were going to kill me anyway I may as well go with my head held up high. Fortunately, my fears were temporarily suspended. I was sentenced to two months in prison, fined one hundred *Louis d'Ors*, and expelled from France within seven days after serving this sentence. I was euphoric to know that I wasn't going to die. Afterwards, I thought how irrational it was to even think that but these were changing times and everyone who didn't fit in was fearful and there were a lot of us for one reason or another."

Leon took another sip of his tea and finished the remainder of his Florentine. He looked around at his family who were sat watching him, waiting on his every word. He wondered if he should have told this story before, or maybe not at all. He had seen things so terrible he didn't think it was right to tell them to other people, let alone his family. He already knew that he had left out things that were too terrible to talk about. The Edelmans had been treated very badly but the night that he decided to leave Berlin, he had seen a Jew he knew from synagogue kicked to death by the Brownshirts for no apparent reason and just left bleeding in the gutter. The Brownshirts were all drunk but knew that nobody cared about the Jews anymore. He had wanted to intervene but knew he would have also been murdered in cold blood. He couldn't tell this to his family.

"Where was I?" he asked, knowing full well where he had left off but he was very pleased that they all quickly reminded him that he was in jail! At least they were listening.

"I was taken back to *La Maison d'Arrêt* manacled to a prison guard and put in a cell in solitary confinement, as I was the only person qualified to be a 'political prisoner'. Life in the prison cells was no picnic. There was little light, little food and no exercise. After a week, I complained and was put in a cell with nine other prisoners, who were jailed for a variety of offences. One of them was charged with being an accessory to murder, while his brother was in another part of the prison sentenced to death for murder. I wondered what on earth I was doing here with hardened criminals when my only crime was not having the correct paperwork. Little did I know at the time that that would be the reason millions were to die over the next six years.

On the first day with my 'new mates', I was not sure that it had been a good idea to be transferred from solitary and I wish I had kept my mouth shut. The regime was that in the daytime we were in one large cell and at night transferred to smaller, more secure, cells (presumably so that some of the guards could go home). We had to undress and hang our day clothes on the rails in the gangway. I asked the other prisoners why they made us do this. So we didn't use them to hang ourselves, they replied. The food was inedible. I was allowed one litre of disgusting wine, which I did not drink or want, but was welcomed by my new friends. This was all quite a shock for a good Jewish boy who had been trying to mind his own business. I had to take great care not to upset any of the other prisoners, who were constantly vying to be top dog. It was a fine line to tread to remain independent but equally to ensure you were supporting the right group. We heard of murders that occurred within the prison, often for retaliation for events that went on outside the prison. I kept myself to myself as much as possible and tried not to rock the boat. Fortunately, as one of the few inmates who could read and write, I was in demand to help with letters to be read and written and was treated with a reasonable amount of civility. This only helped to disguise the reality which was very harsh.

One day, while we were outside exercising in the yard, one of the guys from my cell was stabbed in the stomach. There was blood everywhere and he was screaming with pain. When we tried to go to his aid, the guards kicked us. He was taken away and we never saw him again. Somebody said he had died. A husband, whose wife the prisoner had been seeing, had arranged for the accident to happen. As it turned out, they got the wrong guy, the man they wanted had been freed the day before. By the time I left, four weeks later, the blood was still caked to the concrete in the yard for all to see. That could have been me.

Whilst in prison, I received, from the British Consul General in Paris, confirmation that I had a visa to enter England for one year as a management trainee at the Gaumont Engineering Ltd factory in Finchley. Family contacts in England had arranged for the position and I was relieved. My concern had been that without a position to go to, I might have been arrested again, if not in France then in another country, as the right paperwork was becoming all important in a Europe that was becoming increasingly jittery. The movement of *émigrés* was increasing constantly as the Nazi party exerted influence in all spheres.

After serving my sentence of two months, I returned to Paris and called at the Consulate on La Rue D'Anjou to collect my visa. On that occasion, I was asked very politely why my address was c/o the Prison at Nevers! I explained to the young lady behind the desk, hoping that my story might find a sympathetic ear, especially as she was very pretty and I hadn't seen a girl for over two months, but I didn't get the reaction I was hoping for.

After spending a week in Paris sorting out personal business and saying goodbye to friends, I travelled by train and ferry to England on the 5th July 1939. All the talk, those few days, was about war. Would the Germans invade Poland? I had heard snippets of news whilst in prison but I didn't know how much of it was true. Back in Paris, I followed the newspapers and my friends told me what had been happening."

CHAPTER 5

England, safety and War

"My Uncle Saul met me at Victoria Station. He reminded me of my father and of my family, who I hadn't seen for some time. I had missed them desperately. Imagine my surprise when we arrived at Uncle Saul's apartment and my mother, Alina, and sister, Anna, were already there. They had escaped from Berlin selling everything they could, as had my Uncle Saul. He had a German friend who paid him a much better price than he needed to under the new German laws, for the stock, the shop and my beloved van. This gave the family enough money to buy safe passage and set up home in Essex Road, Islington, London, which is where I stayed for the first few days.

England seemed so different after the previous few months. I felt safe in the leafy streets of Islington. The people were very polite and although there was talk of war, everybody was confident in the British Prime Minister, Neville Chamberlain, agreeing a peace deal with Hitler. Only the year before he had visited Hitler and returned with a paper committing Germany to peace, sadly it turned out to be worthless.

During those early days, I presented myself to the directors of Gaumont Engineering Ltd. I started work within seven days of arriving in England. I had little choice as I was completely without money by now.

This meant that I had to move away from Islington and my newly rediscovered family as it was too far to travel every day. I had no choice under the terms of my visa but to start work immediately. I found a room in a boarding house in Finchley, close to work, with breakfast and dinner included for the princely sum of twenty-five shillings or £1.25 in today's money.

Every morning would be a routine. Mrs Hancock, my landlady, would shout up the stairs, "Aleksandrov, your breakfast's on the table, if you let it go cold that's your problem." Although there were more and more *émigrés* arriving, I was still something of a novelty. They called me the Ruski but never mentioned the fact that I was Jewish, which was refreshing.

Gaumont Engineering was an electrical manufacturing company, specializing in electric irons, heating elements and a number of other accessories. Initially, my work consisted of administration as well as assembly work on the shop floor. We worked five and a half days per week. My wages were one pound a week less one shilling insurance, approximately 95p for fifty hours of work a week, but I was grateful. After the experiences in Berlin, and then Nevers, I was content to be somewhere safe and have some normality, although my basic arithmetic quickly told me that I wouldn't be able to survive financially under the current arrangements. I started to look for work in the evenings teaching German or French or Russian. I was able to travel by omnibus to Islington for a threepenny bit and visit my mother on the weekend.

My search for work did not last long as the

situation in Europe was deteriorating day by day. Within two months of my arrival in England, the Germans invaded Poland on the 1st of September 1939, triggering Britain's involvement in the War as part of a pact with Poland. That same day, I went to the Finchley Recruiting Office and volunteered to join the British Army."

"Why did you join up so quickly, Leon?" asked Paul, who had also come over to join them, along with Anthony, having exhausted the permutations of Chelsea and Arsenals' European football ambitions.

"It was just something that I felt I had to do. I had lived in Poland and felt a part of me was still there. I had also experienced at first-hand what the Nazis were capable of and knew that if we didn't do something to stop them we could all end up being persecuted. I was still Jewish and knew it didn't take much to persuade a whole population to become anti-Semitic.

Anyway, joining up was not as straight-forward as I thought it might have been. In view of the fact that I was Russian born, had arrived in this country from France, but was in fact a refugee from Nazi Germany with a Romanian passport, the War Office Establishment did not know what to do with me, so I had to wait a few months until they decided which unit to place me into, or admit me at all. For the second time in a few months, I was left wondering as to my fate because of my paperwork. As it turned out, I was one of thousands of displaced European refugees who wanted to join up and fight. The problem was not me but what to do with so many of us. There was also a lot of fear about fifth columnists or what you would call spies. When war broke out,

Germans were interned, and later Italians, for fear that they might send sensitive information back; anyone vaguely European was regarded with distrust, England was at war, nobody knew what would happen.

I had to wait but was eventually allowed to join up. I headed off to the Dukes Road in Euston for my Army medical examination. It was a huge, imposing building with a magnificent entrance and I did wonder whether I would pass the medical, even though I thought I was very fit. The corridors were filled with young men of all shapes and sizes. I need not have worried. The examination was so brief; I think as long as you had a pulse you would have been selected. After a long wait, I was called through and met the examining officer and my military records were started. I did not want to be known as Leonid, my birth name, so changed my name to Leon and have been known so ever since.

At the start of the war, the Russians had a non-aggression pact with Germany, so I didn't want a name that sounded so obviously Russian. My height was recorded as 5′ 5¾", weight at 132lbs, complexion fresh, eyes brown, hair brown, Jewish, age approximately twenty-three years with no distinguishing marks. As I did not have a birth certificate, the officer had to take my word for it.

Since 1933, thousands had been arriving from Europe, but especially from Germany, where they had been persecuted. At the outbreak of war there were more than 10,000 of us known as 'Enemy Aliens'. We swore allegiance to King George VI, then volunteered to serve in the British Forces and joined the only unit open to us: the non-combatant Pioneer Corps, known affectionately as 'The King's Most Loyal Enemy Aliens', most of us were Jews, but a significant number were political opponents of the Nazi regime and so-called 'degenerate artists'. With one or two exceptions, we refugees in uniform did not receive British nationality until 1946-7. Because we were all political refugees we were not allowed to join any active units, which we found really upsetting. The British were joining the war to help the persecuted. We were the persecuted but could not join the war. It seemed very strange to us but at the time, as I said, everyone was fearful of spies so you can understand why it was this way. It wasn't just in Germany where people were fearful, it was the same in England, there were spies everywhere, or so people thought. Also, as an island race, the English just weren´t used to seeing all these colourful Europeans and were understandably wary.

Most of these Pioneer Corps were established in remote seaside towns like Westward Ho! in Devonshire. You can imagine how strange it must have been for all of these foreigners and Jews descending on a sleepy Devon seaside town. Many were also stationed in Ilfracombe in north Devon which eventually became home to more than 3,000 Jews. Here, they settled for a time, the majority as refugees in uniform, in former holiday camps or requisitioned hotels. They brought with them a uniquely continental intellect and culture, not only overcoming the natural suspicion of the local population against largely German-speaking refugees, but also coming to terms with their own fears and sense of loss (for many had left families in Europe, never to be seen again). Here I met up with Gerd

Treuhaft, who had left Germany just before war broke out. We had been at school together in Berlin at the Werner Siemens Gymnasium. It was good to see him and we spent lots of time just catching up. It was wonderful to be able to recount stories with an old friend.

We were formed into the Pioneer Company, which had been formed out of the Auxiliary Military Pioneer Corps. As recruits in the Pioneer Corps, we received general military training for a few weeks, although there was no intention by the authorities to use these 'Foreign Legion' units in combat situations. We often discussed whether the British Government just didn't trust us with weapons in case we were some sort of fifth columnists sent here by the Nazis to infiltrate and prepare way for invasion. Our function was to provide support services for the forces, such as loading and unloading railway trucks and lorries with war materials, building, concreting roads, tank parking facilities, building huts for army camps; quite hard work for us, the majority of whom were professional people who had never experienced manual work. Amazingly, ninety-five per cent went to it with great enthusiasm and extraordinary efficiency, achieving record performances and targets. The fact that we were all volunteers and had genuine reasons for wanting to help meant that we were a very focused and useful attribute. Our spirit was really good and there was a great feeling of camaraderie, we were like one big happy family. For many of us who had been constantly displaced throughout our lives, this really was our family.

In November 1940 the Colonel Commandant, Field Marshall Lord Milne, pointed out that the title

Auxiliary Military Pioneer Corps was extremely unpopular with all ranks and bad for morale. At the same time, it was agreed that companies should be fully armed instead of only a quarter of us which had previously been the case. Training centres were quickly formed to receive, clothe and equip recruits, and personnel posted from other companies were formed and dispatched as required. These new companies usually consisted of about 280 men divided into ten sections of twenty-six men and a small HQ. Each section was commanded by a sergeant. Two sections were commanded by a lieutenant. A number of companies (between four and twenty) within a geographical area would be commanded by a Group HQ under a lieutenant colonel. We were transformed in a very short period from a rag tail of *émigrés* into a potential fighting unit. We felt part of the army and part of the struggle. Our numbers were also growing as the situation in Europe worsened and more and more Jews and political and intellectual prisoners escaped.

It was clear to us all that we would be called upon to fight at some stage; the war wasn't always going to be fought on the beaches of England. It is widely thought that all Jews just laid down during the war and were exterminated by the Nazis. This isn't true, many thousands of Jews fought as bravely as many others from the regular army and won a disproportionately large number of medals for valour. I am sure that there were many examples of bravery all over Europe in defiance of the Nazis that were never reported. The odds were always stacked against the Jewish community. Any act of defiance was always countered by extreme violence and retaliation by the *SS*. Many of the Jewish people who were herded into ghettos had families and young children. Fear of seeing their children taken or murdered kept the Jewish community in place.

It was here at Westward Ho! that I met up again with my old friend, Isaak, who had joined another company a few months before me via different channels. It was amazing how our paths kept crossing, but all *émigrés* tended to move in the same straight lines, usually by word of mouth from other *émigrés*. It was good to be involved and trying to make a difference, I had enjoyed my time in Finchley but I knew that this was something I must do. Events in Europe had denied me a home and my family; this was my chance to do something about that. We picked up where we had left off and even met up with some other friends from Berlin. Isaak had also known Gerd, so the three of us would go out together. Our community was very tight knit and we all had stories to tell, how we had escaped, those we left behind. We were lucky to be relatively free as we all knew friends and family who had not made it.

Some of our friends would receive letters from Europe, generally it was bad news, mostly of families losing their homes and being forced to move, stripped of their possessions. Jews had become second class citizens and had lost all their rights. We all knew more and more friends and family who were being removed to concentration camps or taken to ghettos. We all knew how lucky we were to have got out when we did. Sometimes we felt guilty, as we sat in a comfortable pub drinking beer, knowing the fate that had befallen friends and family, but we tried to remain positive. Of course at that time everyone was still worried about the Germans invading England. We didn't really have any thoughts that one day we might be able to return to Germany, there was real fear that England could fall.

Isaak and I spent the first year in Devon. It was relatively boring and relentless work. The news was not good at that time. Poland was invaded and then Holland, Belgium and Luxembourg, pretty soon it was France's turn. We sent an army to Europe to help, which was called the British Expeditionary Force, but it had been immediately repelled by the Germans. Although we were lucky to get 340,000 men off the beaches and back to England, the army had lost so much equipment and it was going to take a long time to re-equip and re-organise.

Not soon afterwards, Winston Churchill became Prime Minister, but at that time all the news was bad, the Nazis seemed unstoppable.

The summer of 1940 was the Battle of Britain, when a small group of fighter pilots held back the might of the German Luftwaffe. One of the most distinguished squadrons were the 302 and 303 squadrons which were Polish. We followed their exploits all of the time. Of course, there was so much propaganda, so you couldn't always believe what you read in the papers, but we were used to that, having grown up with the Nazi propaganda machine. There was always someone who knew a Pole in the squadron or a friend. Their success was incredible and was helping us as the British Government realized that the Foreign Legions could be of real use after all. The English fighter squadrons were amazed at the bravery of the Polish fighters, who would get within one hundred yards of the German planes before shooting, even though the Royal Air Force pilots had been taught to open fire at four hundred yards. At first, they were considered crazy, but when their kills mounted up, the English respected them and changed the way they themselves operated. It was a significant event for us displaced fighters. I think the Government also realized that we had even better reasons to fight harder than anyone else as we had already lost everything.

These were terrible times. Not everything was being reported in the newspapers for fear of starting a panic, so we relied on bits of news coming back through the military. There was a feeling that nothing could stop the Nazi war machine and we discussed where else we could flee to, if the Germans took over Britain, knowing that as Jews we would be persecuted or worse, although in the end we all agreed that we would fight to the death and make this our last stand. I know that this must sound so dramatic now as we all sit here enjoying Christmas together, but nobody knew what was going to happen next."

***

"What's happening here?" asked Donna. She and Roger had opened two bottles of Champagne they had brought as Roger always liked to show off a little bit. This always embarrassed Donna as she, Susan and Jane always discussed the food and drink before the families got together to spread the work and the expense, but Roger couldn't help himself.

"Dad is just telling us about his time in the war," said Anthony.

"Why have you never spoken about it before?"

asked Jane.

"It was something very personal, almost another time, a different world. It is so difficult to describe the way things were when today everyone takes their lives for granted. When you don't know if you will be alive next week, or next month, your attitude to life changes. Not just for me but for everyone," replied Leon.

"Come on everyone," said Roger. "A glass of champagne to celebrate Christmas and being together, just a little treat from Donna and myself. What is it you all say? *L'Chaim?*"

"To Life," shouted everyone in unison.

"*Budmo*," shouted Pepe.

"Health and Happiness."

Everyone chinked their glasses and took a sip, eager to return to the story.

"Come and sit down, Donna, this is so interesting." said Jane. "Roger, come and sit next to me."

"Just let me turn the oven down, sis, I won't be a minute." A moment later Donna returned and sat down in the only space left on the sofa, next to Paul. The whole family now formed in an arc around Pepe, the storyteller.

"Carry on, Pepe," said Olivia.

"Where was I?" asked Pepe.

"You were talking about the Battle of Britain and the Polish pilots, I didn´t even know that the Poles flew planes in the war for us," said Jonathan.

"I am not sure they were flying the planes for you! They had just lost their country and were trying to do what they could, we all were, but I suppose we were all in it together, there was a great feeling of camaraderie which was comforting.

Isaak and I were moved to Long Eaton, situated between Nottingham and Derby. We travelled there by train. It was dreadful at the various railway stations en route with children on the platforms with labels around their necks to identify them as part of the evacuation of the cities. All the road signs were removed in case the Germans invaded. It was very strange, but also very depressing. The summer passed and the invasion didn't come, our fighter pilots won the Battle of Britain. Sometimes we saw dogfights above us and on one occasion we were sat in the beer garden of a pub and saw a Spitfire chasing a Heinkel across the sky, the two of them in and out of the clouds with us all cheering the Spitfire pilot on. We saw him pass the lumbering German bomber a couple of times opening fire and after a few minutes we saw smoke bellow out of one of the Heinkel's engines and it started to bank so we could see the whole plane at ninety degrees with its very distinctive glass nose. Three airmen tumbled out and their parachutes opened straight away. We were all cheering but of course this plane had a crew of five so two didn't make it. The Spitfire came round once more and flew past the parachutes tipping its wings as it flew past. The pilot probably saw us all in the pub waving. The whole pub went wild! We could see the German plane come down in the distance into some fields and saw the explosion about a mile away. The parachutes were landing only a couple of fields away from the pub so we all started to run over, this was much more excitement than a lot of people had seen for some time and remember that most British people had never met a German and were very curious especially considering the propaganda.

As we approached the field, about a dozen of us, we could see the German airmen gathering their parachutes. They came together and stood there nervously. A local policeman had also arrived on his bike and there was a momentary stand-off as everyone including the Germans wondered what we should do next. One of the German's took a pistol from his flying suit and everybody jumped back but he immediately turned it around and tried to hand it to Isaak and I as we were in uniform. Fortunately I spoke German and was able to help the police officer take the surrender of the three German airmen. Everyone was very nervous and even looked at me quite strangely because I spoke German, at that time very few English people spoke a foreign language. I asked the policeman what we should do with them. He said that he needed to make a telephone call to have them picked up so we all marched them back to the pub being the nearest building where there was a phone. Isaak and I chatted to the three airmen who were all very nice young men. The captain was from Cologne, his co-pilot and gunner from Hamburg. They seemed quite relieved that their war was over and were saddened at the loss of their friends, the other two crew who hadn't made it out of the burning plane. Everyone was asking us what we were talking to them about so I said we were interrogating them about their intentions but actually they were just telling us about their families. It was understandable why everyone was so terrified of these Germans with their flying kit, goggles and air-tanks, they looked and sounded like aliens. The English press had also made the Germans out to be terrible people as well, so the whole situation was quite surreal. At one stage I thought the policeman was going to arrest us too.

Chatting to them, they were convinced that Germany was going to win the war that it was only a matter of time but they seemed genuinely saddened to be fighting the British whom they respected. I told them that all the soldiers from Europe were now in England and that we had an army ten times the size of the Third Reich and that they would never take England, that all their planes would get shot down. I don't know if they believed me or not.

When we arrived at the pub we sat them down in the beer garden whilst the policeman went and made his call. I asked the landlord to bring them a beer each to which there was a great commotion so I asked those around how they would like our airmen to be treated if they were shot down over Germany. With some reluctance the Landlord brought over five pints of warm English beer for the remains of the Heinkel crew and Isaak and myself. We sat there, two enemy nations enjoying a pint of beer together with thirty or so locals watching us like fish in a bowl and exotic fish to boot.

Half an hour later two army lorries arrived with a whole platoon and a commanding officer who took the Germans away. As they boarded the lorry they saluted me and in broken English said 'thank you' to the crowd gathered to which someone replied 'your war's over, Adolf!' to hoots of laughter."

"That's amazing" said Anthony. It was pretty clear that everyone thought the same from their reactions.

"It was quite an event I must admit but turned out to be quite tame compared to what was to come. At least it was a moment of excitement to break up the boredom of that time.

The accommodation at Long Eaton was worse than in Devon. We continued with our basic work and training through the autumn into winter and it was very cold. Every day was sub-zero. Our hastily assembled Nissan hut was damp; the ice formed on the inside of the windows and the work was boring. We were getting restless. All we wanted to do was fight; we couldn't understand why we were still loading, unloading and digging. The summer of 1940 had been very hot and when we had won the Battle of Britain we thought that would be the tide turning on the war, but it wasn't the case, boredom was by far the worst thing.

In January 1941, Isaak's army girlfriend, Peggy, organized a blind date with another army girlfriend of hers. Isaak and I went to our local pub, The Wheatsheaf, where we met his girlfriend and her friend, Evelyn. Peggy was a lovely girl that Isaak had met on the first day we moved to Long Eaton. Her friend Evelyn was an extremely attractive brunette with a fabulous figure and a very pretty smile. We had a wonderful evening and, for the first time in a long while, I forgot about the war, captivated by her smile and bright blue eyes. Evelyn told me all about her childhood, her life as a Yorkshire girl from Harrogate and how she had quickly joined up with the WAAF, The Women's Auxiliary Air Force when war broke out. I told her all about my life travelling across Europe, escaping from Berlin, my prison spell in Nevers. She thought my life was very exotic. Perhaps it sounded that way, even though I had always felt as though I was on the move and living out of a suitcase. I envied her cosy family life with her parents, school and friends.

The evening went so fast. Evelyn was only nineteen and I was twenty-three, but she was very mature for her age, but then so was everyone, that was quite a time for growing up quickly. She had a very infectious laugh; I seem to recall we spent the whole evening laughing about something or other. It was such a relief for us, as our world seemed so dull at that time. Evelyn was a breath of fresh air, colourful and bright in a world that seemed so black and white or at least olive drab.

We were the last four in the pub and the landlord rang his bell and asked us to leave. He had allowed us to stay long after closing time, huddled by the fire, this was not uncommon at that time, to allow servicemen and servicewomen to stay on later and, as Isaak and I frequented this particular pub quite often, he knew us well.

Outside, the snow was gently falling and there was a full moon which lit up Evelyn's face as we walked the girls back to their home. After that first kiss, I knew I would make Evelyn my wife. It was the start of a very intense and passionate courtship. It is funny to think that without Isaak´s girlfriend arranging that blind date, none of you would be sat here today. I think we should raise our glasses to Peggy!"

"To Peggy," they all chimed in unison as they chinked their champagne glasses for the second time.

"A few months later I got notice that my unit was being moved from Long Eaton. We had no say in these matters; they were the orders and had to be followed. It was difficult to keep our courtship going as our days off or weekends did not always coincide, but telephone and letters kept us in touch and some of our leave could be arranged at the same time. We persevered, during the frequent separations.

It was so hard, so very hard to endure. It was the same for Isaak and Peggy and on a few occasions where leave coincided, the four of us were able to meet up together. Isaak and I had had two more moves spending the whole of our Pioneer Corps Service together, until May 1943, when we both volunteered to join the Royal Armoured Corps and were transferred to a training regiment in Farnborough until July 1943. In 1942, the Government had allowed the 'Enemy Aliens' to join fighting units. This was great news for all of us displaced Jews. It was bad enough not having a home, or even a homeland, but worse still was the fact that we couldn't fight. We were some of the most motivated soldiers and I think in the end the Ministry of War realized that, they also knew it was going to take every able bodied man to beat down the door on 'Fortress Europe', as it was now known.

This was now a very different experience. We were being treated as soldiers and trained accordingly and we trained with relish. The war was beginning to change, the Germans had been defeated at Stalingrad and the North Africa campaign was won. The Americans had joined the war after the Japanese attack on Pearl Harbour, there had even been a Jewish uprising in the ghetto in Warsaw.

In our unit in Farnborough there were many Jews. We were all so happy to hear this news and just wanted our turn to get back at the Nazis. We were hearing terrible stories in the letters we received from family but at that time nobody knew about the concentration camps. The previous two years had dragged. All I could think about was the next time I would see Evelyn, my life was punctuated between the never ending and boring tasks the officers would give us and the times I would see your mother and grandmother." Leon looked at all his family sat before him and smiled.

"Isaak and I knew that it wouldn't be long until there was an invasion of Europe. Neither of us knew if we would come back, so I decided to ask Evelyn to marry me. On a furlough, I met Evelyn in the Hertfordshire countryside. I had packed a picnic and we took a walk from the railway station and sat under an oak tree. It was early June and we basked in the warm sunshine, enjoying our picnic. I had saved all of my ration coupons so we could have a little meat and cheese with our bread and a small bottle of wine. I had tried to get champagne but it was impossible. Evelyn said yes when I asked her and we cried with happiness. We knew it was more symbolic than just getting married. We both knew that I was joining the invasion and neither of us could know what lay ahead. This was the same for every young couple at that time. We made the day last as long as possible and stood holding each other on the platform until the train was leaving that evening. It was very emotional. As we said goodbye to each other, bombers were passing overhead on their way to Germany.

We had to marry quickly because I was being transferred to the Royal Armoured Corps. We married on the 18th of June 1943 at the Kings Road, London Registry Office, the same one that is there today. It was a very wet day and we were totally soaked in our uniforms. There was no wedding dress or smart suit. We only had two witnesses present, my good friend Isaak, of course, and my cousin Olga. I know it is hard to imagine when today at a wedding there might be hundreds of guests, but at that time everyone was displaced, in units all over the country and of course there was no way we could have a wedding reception, there was rationing and it was all very difficult. It was hard enough getting a two day pass to even get married!"

"Did you go on honeymoon?" asked Anthony.

"Ha ha," laughed Leon. "A honeymoon! We were able to book one night in a hotel in Paddington. We had fish and chips with Isaak and your Great Aunt Olga. Fish and chips were one of the only things you could buy without coupons. The fish and chip shops only opened a few days a week, although potatoes were plentiful with everyone growing them in their gardens, fish was harder to come by, as many fishing vessels were now working for the Royal Navy. We had a celebratory drink in a pub, that was our wedding reception, and our honeymoon was one night at the Railway Hotel in Paddington. Even that was disturbed by an air raid and we had to spend half the night in Paddington Tube! The following day, I met Isaak on the platform where I said goodbye to Evie, as you knew her, not knowing when we would see each other again. Isn't it funny, the thing I most remember about that moment was, when we kissed goodbye, we both laughed because our uniforms were still damp, even though we had tried to dry them out on the hotel radiators. Everything seemed strangely comical.

Even though I had just married, I was not allowed any additional leave and nor was Evie. We had to snatch moments together when we could.

Isaak and I returned to Farnborough, where we were doing our training, and then were moved to Aldershot, where we were transferred to front line regiments. Evelyn returned to her unit in Leicestershire. Isaak and I joined the 8th Kings Royal Irish Hussars within the 7th Armoured Division also known as the Desert Rats. They came with quite a reputation, having defeated Rommel in North Africa. They had seen a lot of fighting and were used to hardship, so initially the veterans didn't give us new recruits the time of day, we had to really prove ourselves."

"I have heard of them," said Jonathan. "We studied them in history, they fought in North Africa at Tobruk and El Alamein against Rommel, that was really interesting."

"That's right," said Pepe. "But by this time, the war in North Africa was over. Rommel had been beaten at El Alamein and many of the Desert Rats returned home to form new units ready for the invasion. Some of them had even fought in the allied invasion of Italy in September 1943.

We were transferred to West Tofts in Norfolk, where the whole regiment was being reformed. We were now training and working with soldiers who had seen real combat; their stories were frightening, but exciting. We were preparing in an area known as the Stanford Battle Area. Because we were using live ammunition, a thousand residents were relocated, which must have been hard for them. I was acutely aware of the hardship we were putting on people, making them move, and of course it reminded me of the Edelmans in Berlin. I am sure those that were made to move from West Tofts were compensated and they were able to return after we left, so it wasn't quite as bad.

Of course, I missed your grandmother desperately, we hardly saw each other during this time but the training was so exciting, it kept me busy and my mind off my new wife.

At West Tofts, we were trained in the new Cromwell tanks equipped with 75mm guns. It was really exciting driving them, firing off rounds of live ammunition, blowing things up. Of course it was quite easy because there wasn't anyone firing back.

Every man was trained in a particular discipline, in my case as a tank driver, but every man had to be accomplished in gunnery, wireless operation and machine guns. The training was relentless, we had a genuine feeling that a big push was coming. At that time, we heard that lots of Americans were arriving in England and had their own training camps, so we knew something big was happening but it was all being kept a big secret to retain the element of surprise. We only found out after the war how much of a secret it really had been, using double agents to throw the Germans off the scent. They really thought we were invading somewhere else which saved a lot of lives. The Intelligence Services even created a fictitious American army.

The arrival of the Americans had another impact. The Americans were very well supplied compared to us. They had unlimited amounts of cigarettes, more money and access to things like food we hadn't seen for a while, as well as nylons for the ladies. Do you know they were paid five times what we were earning in the army? This made them very popular amongst British women. One of the great unspoken truths about the war was the boredom that so many people experienced. With so many of the young men away, women were bored. We would sometimes go to a dance and there would be a hundred women but only ten men. The women would often dance with each other just for something different to do to relieve the monotony of working in the factories or on the land, as all the women had to contribute to the war effort. You can imagine when all of these bright faced, young, American GIs turned up, the women were very excited. You probably heard the phrase 'overpaid, oversexed and over here', well the Americans used to describe us as 'underpaid, undersexed and under Eisenhower!' and they were probably right!

News quickly got around about liaisons that were happening between the GIs and the British women. This was not very popular, especially when some of the women were married and their husbands had been away for some time. It wasn't long until babies were appearing and that's when it got really difficult. It was a fear that many British soldiers had that their wives or girlfriends might have a fling with an American, and who could blame them?

These were tedious times. Nobody was able to build their lives; everything was on hold just trying to win the war and with no idea of the outcome. People took solace where they could; it is difficult to comprehend today.

One of the other big shocks that happened with the arrival of the Americans was the arrival of their black troops. About 100,000 of them arrived in the UK during the war, compared to only about 7,000 black people who lived here at the time. As if that wasn't a big shock, the American black troops were all segregated. This was long before Martin Luther King and long before mass immigration to the UK, which started after the war. We are now an integrated multi-cultural society but at that time it was an enormous shock, especially if you were a small town or village in the English countryside and a whole regiment of black soldiers were billeted there. There were many British people who had never seen a black man before and their first experience was that they were treated differently by their white American counterparts," said Leon.

"I didn't realize there were so few black people living in England," said Claudia. "That is amazing, so all the immigration happened after the war?"

"Yes, that's right, the world changed completely during the war. So many people had travelled and there was such a need for labour in the reconstruction process. The Commonwealth had been united behind the effort to defeat the Nazis and Japan which meant that freedom of movement was actually encouraged. Britain had already had an influx of refugees from Europe, like me and Isaak, so attitudes had changed. Immigration really took off after the war. It is wonderful that you have grown up so used to seeing many different people, all colours and religions, but that wasn't the case prior to the war; there really had been very little immigration apart from Europeans.

Anyway, back to my story. By now we had become the Armoured Reconnaissance regiment of the 7th Armoured Division. I was part of a five man crew and we had to learn how to manage our new batch of Cromwell tanks that had just been delivered. My crew consisted of my commanding officer, Harry Fathers, a very pleasant twenty-five year old, who had experience in the North Africa campaign. He wasn't as battle weary as others and treated the rest of us as equals. He commanded from the turret along with the gunner, Ishmael, a Jewish immigrant who had fled from Poland, and his loader François, who had escaped Paris the same time as I had.

He was a little older and had been a professor at a University. He had been writing inflammatory articles about the French Government and their attitude towards the Jews. In the front of the hull was a gunner, who manned the machine guns. His name was Albrecht. He had escaped from Cologne in Germany in early 1941 by walking all the way to Switzerland. He had abandoned everything. All the Jews had been herded into two blocks and were about to be loaded onto trains. Albrecht had the state of mind to knock down a wall and escape into the night. He told us one night over a few beers that he did this with three friends that he had known since his school days. They had ignored what the older Jewish members of their community had said. Even at that point many of the older people thought that the Germans would still look after them and they were indeed being transferred to a work camp where if they worked they would be fed.

Albrecht and his friends were having none of it. They had spotted a weakness in a wall that had been damaged by allied bombing and smashed it down, fleeing into the night with a couple of loaves of bread. Almost as soon as they were on the other side, the German guards spotted them and opened up. All three of his friends were shot. Albrecht just kept running and escaped, hiding in a cellar covered in coal. He could hear the guards and the dogs outside looking for him. The following night, he emerged and spent the next three weeks walking until eventually he found himself at the border of Switzerland. He had his mother's jewellery in his pocket, which he used to bribe the border guards to allow him in. After that, he contacted the British Embassy who arranged for passage for him to England, but only after lengthy interrogation. There was always the risk that the Germans would try to plant spies in this way. Albrecht had eventually found his way to us and his stories kept us fascinated. He had really experienced the nightmare of the Nazis at first hand. He later found out that all of his family had died at Treblinka concentration camp so he, like all of us, was desperate to get to Europe and get his revenge.

In the six months that we trained together, the five of us became very close friends. We spent all day every day (apart from the brief amount of leave that we were allowed) in each other's company, working, eating, laughing, telling stories and a lot of the time within the close confines of the tank itself, five completely different individuals thrown together. In any other circumstances I am sure we would have fallen out but we had one goal and that made us very close. I became very attached to Albrecht, who we nicknamed Shorty because he was over six feet tall and was always cramped in the gunnery position. Being in a tank crew suited being shorter, like myself. He used to joke that one day he would be the commander and could stick his head out of the top of the turret like Harry, but we all said that the minute he did that he would get his head blown off.

As our training progressed, we started the last

stage, which was underwater landing procedures. This was quite a hazardous undertaking at Lowestoft, where the beaches were flat and the water shallow, so we had to start a long way out to sea. We had received the new '*Schnorkel*' device and we were given the task of testing it out first. This was an attachment that was designed to allow the tank to travel a short distance underwater whilst allowing air into the tank and the engine to continue running. Why we were given this dubious honour I am not sure, perhaps because we had performed well in all the other tasks.

The engineers who had been sent from the factory to fit it talked us through how it should work. They installed all of the various pipes and pumps. We had a short-wave radio to tell them how it was performing whilst we were going through the test. We loaded our tank into an American built landing craft and went three hundred yards out to sea. The sea was quite calm that day but the landing craft, because of its flat hull, was lurching from side to side. The captain of the craft turned inwards and started heading for land. He told us to be ready and that we were two minutes away. We closed all the hatches and switched on the pumps. We could see the front ramp lower and I pushed the gears forwards and our tank rolled out of the craft and sank towards the bottom of the sea. It was still relatively shallow but almost the whole tank was submerged. We were all very nervous.

'Let's go, Leon,' shouted Harry and I pushed the gears forwards and we set off towards the beach. The optimum speed we were told was eight miles an hour. After a few seconds, water started leaking into the hull through one of the pipes. Harry started shouting at me to speed up, as did Shorty, Ishmael and

François. There was pandemonium in the tank as the water started rising and was already up to our knees and gushing in through the pipe. I sped the tank up to as fast as it would go but this only helped the water to come in faster because the pump was actually connected to our engine for power.

The water was rising even faster and was now up to our waists. Harry was shouting, saying that we would have to abandon the tank, but I kept driving forwards and within a few more seconds, sky started to appear above us and we ran out and up onto the beach. The water started to drain away out of the tank and very shortly we were up on dry land. We threw open the hatches and clambered out, gasping for air. The engineers and a whole throng of other tank crews came running up to us.

'Couldn't you hear us on the radio?' they asked. 'We could hear all the commotion in your tank and were trying to tell you what to do.' In all the commotion, Shorty hadn't thought to turn the switch to hear what they were saying. We had just needed to switch one of the valves to overcome the problem. We never let him forget that! We were given a pass out of the camp that night and Albrecht bought us all beers and we joked about the day saying that we had better get it right if we ever did get to Europe. We were quite a crew, great friends brought together in adversity.

Evie and I did get to see each other once a month, but only fleetingly. We could only ever get a two day pass and it took more than a day for us both to get there and back wherever we arranged to meet, but it meant we looked so forward to meeting each other and we wrote every single day. There were so many relationships being conducted like this at that time. Isaak had the same problem with Peggy, so we could console ourselves. I know that today all of you young people communicate by the internet and mobile phones with messages, we had letters, and I have kept them all here in my satchel.

The training continued and we wanted to get in amongst the Nazis but of course by now it was winter and a European invasion was out of the question, the weather was just too bad to put that many troops on the water. We later found out that the invasion couldn't have been planned until we had won the Battle of the Atlantic so that the Americans could safely build up their forces in Britain, but the British and Americans were under pressure from Russia to start a second front. The Russians were suffering terrible losses in the east and they needed us to take some of the pressure off. The Allied invasion in Italy had helped but there was a desperate need to start a front in France.

The year seemed to drag on, illuminated by the snatched moments Evie and I spent together. By April 1944, the invasion was on. It was still meant to be very secret but we all knew what was coming. Everyone was just waiting for the right weather. The last days of May and the first days of June 1944, units of all services were moved to the south coast ready for the invasion of France.

Evie and I organized a final meeting before I was due to leave. We didn't know the exact day of my departure but a week before, what was to become the D-Day landings, we met in London. We both had a night pass and were able to return to the Paddington Station hotel where we spent our honeymoon. That evening there were no air raids and we were able to say goodbye properly. We didn't really talk about very much at all; it was hard to know what to say. We didn't know when we would meet each other again or even if I would ever come back. Evie gave me her scarf, which I kept with me every day and still have here in my satchel."

Leon pulled out a small silk scarf, it was very faded and worn, it looked as though it had been to war.

"I know it sounds crazy, but sometimes this scarf just kept me going, it always reminded me of your grandmother. We said goodbye on the platform of Paddington station. It seemed that our whole relationship had revolved around farewells on station platforms. There were dozens of other couples there at the same time doing the same thing, a mass of olive drab and uniforms, kissing farewell by waiting trains. We were nothing unusual. We hadn't made any of the usual plans that a young couple might make. We never discussed getting a house together or starting a family. Only a few years before we thought we might be invaded and taken over by the Nazis. We just tried to live every day as though it were our last with no plans for the future, we didn't know if we had a future."

Leon's eyes glazed over and a tear built up in the corner of his right eye, under his glasses, dropping onto his cheek. He quickly wiped it away with his hand, it was clear for everyone to see that this was quite draining for the old man.

"Are you ok, Pepe? Why don't you take a break?" asked Hannah.

"I will be fine, there is so much to tell you, I have hardly begun!" he replied.

CHAPTER 6

D-Day June 6th 1944

"Almost as soon as I returned to base, we were moved to Gosport near Portsmouth. Some of us went by train, others by lorry. I went by train, as I had to drive my tank off the train at the other end. The High Command didn't want tanks travelling by road as there were German spotter planes above, so they put them on trains and camouflaged them. Everything was done to try and deceive the Germans as to what we were doing, although how they could hide the hundreds of thousands of troops gathering in the ports on the south coast and all the boats, I don't know.

The deception went as far as Eisenhower attending the 1944 Cup Final between Chelsea and Charlton Athletic at Wembley, giving the impression that the invasion was not imminent. They had deceived the Germans into thinking the invasion was going to be in the Pas De Calais area eventually, so I suppose the Germans would have expected the troops to be on the south coast anyway. I said farewell to my chums and drove our tank to the station not far from Lowestoft. There was so much excitement on the train. We were all talking about getting to Berlin and how it would all be over by Christmas. I was reunited on the train journey with Gerd Treuhaft. We had exchanged some letters but hadn't seen each other for almost two years. He was also a driver of a Cromwell tank.

When we arrived in Portsmouth it was organized chaos. On the first day of the landings, 155,000 troops were shipped across the English Channel and landed with all of their equipment, so you can imagine how many people there were crammed into all the ports along the south coast.

A day before embarkation, I was ordered to proceed to the Forward Tank Delivery depot to collect a new tank. I don't know why I was singled out for this. I met with my new tank crew and spent a couple of hours checking over the new vehicle, making sure I was familiar with it. It was brand new and had probably come straight to the port from the factory so I didn't even know if it had been properly tested. It was a Cromwell and identical in every way to the one I had been training on for months, the only difference was it smelt of new paint and did not feel like home. The tank we had been training in was festooned with our pictures and writing on the walls. This was completely against military discipline but it was common amongst tank crews to personalise their tanks.

That last evening in Portsmouth, I tried to find Harry, Albrecht, François and Ischmael, but with no success. I knew they were somewhere in the area but the place was boiling over with men and equipment and it was almost impossible to move freely. Apart from the vast numbers, the Military Police were questioning everyone, asking for ID constantly so movement was prohibited. I wanted to see my friends before we set off, just in case anything should happen.

I embarked for the invasion of France on an American tank landing craft, which itself was loaded into a very large vessel. I was separated from my own regiment. I didn't like this at all, we had all become great friends and I wanted to fight with them and if necessary die with them too, not just my tank crew but the rest of the 'enemy aliens'. We had been together for two years and I was quite upset, but the fear of the day ahead kept me focused.

I had been issued with a ration pack, enough for two days in the event of being separated at landing. Nobody knew what to expect.

We left Bumper Quay in a naval convoy at eleven a.m. on the 7th June, heading for the Normandy beaches. We were in the second wave of the invasion, the initial landings being on the 6th June. We assumed that the Germans would be bringing up reinforcements and that we could expect a hostile reception. The journey across the English Channel was not too rough but lots of people were being sick, a combination of seasickness and nerves. The smell was horrendous as others had lost their composure.

A young man opposite me, no more than eighteen years of age, was very ill. He held a picture in his hand, I think it was of his mother and was then sick all over my boots. He tried to apologise but it didn't matter. Some men were boisterous, even able to eat, while others were very quiet, we all handled the situation in our own way. I was thinking about Evie, remembering the day under the oak tree in Hertfordshire, the sunlight, the warmth, her beautiful hair. I remember gripping her scarf in my pocket.

As we approached the beach, we were ordered into our tanks, which had been pre-loaded into the landing craft. I didn't know my new crew; we had only met the evening before. I had driven onto the vessel myself and had not sat with them during the crossing. We clambered into the tight space together, virtually silent. We all knew what we had to do. The landing craft were released. These were flat bottomed vessels with no keel, identical to the ones we had used in training in West Tofts, which immediately started rolling in the sea, enemy fire came in and shells were exploding in the sea all around us. We were trying to land at Arromanche with support from the 47th and 50th Commandos on Gold beach. The landing was supposed to be at low tide to negate Rommel's defences planned for a high tide offensive but the wind was bringing the tide in from west to east, we couldn't see the defences. Our tanks were fitted with the '*Schnorkel*' device we had trained with. It had been modified during the previous few months and was much improved. As soon as the vehicle mounted the beach, at the driver's controls, was a special lever, which released the '*Schnorkel*' equipment which dropped off onto the sand.

The area we were landing in was five miles wide. As we approached the beach we could see almost the full length of the attack area. We were more or less in the middle. We could see other landing craft blowing up as they hit mines or took a direct hit, or getting stuck on the underwater defences and men drowning, weighed down by their equipment. On the journey in to the beaches that was our greatest fear, ending up in the water unable to take off the equipment fast enough and being dragged to the ocean bed and drowning. Having seen what happens to the human body when it takes a direct hit from machine gun fire,

I would have taken the drowning option anytime.

The engineers ahead of us were trying to blow up the underwater defences but were being strafed by the Germans from the beaches. We lost a number of tanks before they even got to the beach and the engineers took a real hammering. Shells were landing everywhere and we were very fearful but the adrenalin just kept us going. I prayed that our tank would keep running; bearing in mind I didn't know this tank, having only seen it for the first time the day before. Machine gun bullets were ricocheting off the armour and I wondered what the chances were of a bullet getting through the drivers slit I was using to see where I was going. The engineers had cleared some of the tank traps, creating a small entrance on to the beach, which unfortunately was attracting all of the fire. We clambered onto the French sand and accelerated off, firing as we went through the first gap.

As I steered, I tried to avoid the bodies that were before us, not knowing if the soldiers were dead or wounded. It was bedlam, we didn't have any orders and couldn't receive any, the radio was just a crackling fuzz. Our gunner was training on a concrete gun emplacement high on the buff above us. Before we could get off a round, the gun emplacement just blew up and disappeared. By now, our warships had the range and were starting to pick off the German guns. We still had the problems of machine guns strafing the beaches and pinning the commandos down and German mortars were also playing havoc. The beach had already had a pounding from our ships and some forward units had cleared the beach of mines, but there were still plenty of tank traps, and other defences to avoid, that Rommel had ordered. One of these was known as 'Rommel's asparagus' which was designed to spear paratroopers. Some of it was really quite medieval, sharpened logs and bits of metal.

We started to fight our way off the beach driving the Germans back, shelling their gun emplacements and machine gunning ahead, clearing the way for our commandos to push forwards. Our own soldiers were walking behind the tanks, trying to get some cover on the beach. I tried to pick my way through the mess and debris that was everywhere. Suddenly, a shell landed directly in front of us. I didn't know where it had come from, whether it was from one of our battleships or a German anti-tank gun or even a mine.

The sand blew up and over the tank, flying in through the driver's slit. I had sand in my eyes, stinging dreadfully, and I couldn't see. I tried to rub them but the sand was too painful. As I leant down to grab my water bottle, I felt the tank lurch forwards suddenly and tip earthwards almost at ninety degrees. Although I couldn't see, I could tell that we had driven into the hole created by the explosion and that our tank was probably wedged in an almost upright position. Immediately, I could hear machine gun fire ricocheting off the turret. We were a sitting target. I put my hands out, wondering where my bottle could have fallen to. At that moment, Joe, my gunner, realizing what had happened, thrust his bottle into my hands.

I threw the contents into my face and tried to wash the sand out. It was stinging like hell and the noise of the bullets bouncing off our tank was getting louder and more constant. I knew that I had to get us moving, and fast, before an anti-tank gun has us in its sights. After a third attempt, I managed to dislodge enough sand to see what I was doing. I quickly found the gears and started to shunt so that the tracks caught a grip and, after a few jerks, we had bounced down into the shell hole and were coming out the other side.

Pietre, who was a Romanian refugee, was by now firing rounds from our 75mm cannon at a constant velocity as we rushed forwards. Our soldiers behind us firing over the top of the tank at the same time, we must have created quite some firepower. The machine gunning that had been hammering our tank suddenly stopped and we knew that at least one German machine gun nest was no more.

I saw an incline off the beach to the left and headed for it. There were already tank tracks there so I could hopefully assume that we were not the first tank to travel up there and hopefully there would not be any mines. As we rushed up the bank and over the dunes we could see Germans fleeing from their gun emplacements. Our troops from the back of the tank quickly rounded up those that surrendered; anyone who tried to fire back was quickly dispatched. We had about twenty German prisoners to look after and were waiting for orders. We could see fighting going on all along the beach, some areas were clearly very fierce, with additional support coming from our destroyers at sea and air support.

The landing went on for many hours as the Germans threw everything they had at us. We took a lot of casualties but as we found later, nothing like the Americans at Omaha beach. They had a torrid time and lost 5,000 out of their 50,000 complement so we were relatively lucky, although we still had four hundred men lost or injured. We kept pushing forwards. As the Germans took their own casualties and reduced their firepower, we were able to get round the flanks and take out the last of the gun emplacements, bunkers and machine gun nests. The defences had been strong but these were not the elite troops of the *Waffen SS* or the Panzer divisions.

Unknown to us, we had been pounded on the beach by a battery of four 155mm guns a kilometre inland who had been directed by an observation post on the beach. HMS Ajax had taken these guns out in a fierce dual. It was probably these guns that had blown the hole we were nearly trapped in. A few yards longer and we would have been blown to smithereens and none of you would be here today. By the end of the day we had secured the beachhead and were taking a well-earned break, having achieved almost all of our objectives. All of my crew were fine, shaken but elated and the tank had held up well despite being hit by machine gun fire. There was no enemy armour on the beach but it had still been one hell of a fight.

Joe, Pietre and I sat on our tank. We had been through hell but had come out unscathed. We were perched at the top of a small dune next to a shattered German battery. As we looked back at the beach we could see an awful scene; bodies and limbs in our green uniforms and the same in the German blue uniforms. The colour may have been different but they were still flesh and blood like us. What on earth was it for? All that death and destruction on a beach that none of us had ever been to before. We couldn't talk to one another, we knew how lucky we had been. We had been protected by thick armour plate. The medics were treating the injured close to us in a medical unit that had been hastily assembled. The screams of pain were horrific even though we were all still partly deaf from the repeated explosions during our assault.

Joe passed round his cigarettes and we all sat there together in silence thinking about what we had seen and what we had done. For the first and last time, I thought about the Germans that we killed that day. I knew that I could not think about that again. We were a long way from Germany and this was not going to be the only day we would be firing at them, trying to stay alive. I had to rationalize it in my own mind that it was us or them. I thought about the *Gestapo* and what had happened in Berlin before I left; the news we had heard about family and friends losing their homes, I knew that I could not make this war personal. I had a job to do and could not think of the enemy as human. It would be impossible to go into battle worrying about the other side. I think every man on the beach that day must have had the same thoughts.

I was given orders to re-join my regiment. I reported to the newly set up headquarters for the 7th Armoured Division, which was only a mile from where we had been resting. As soon as I walked into the tent and saw my commanding officer, Captain Hillier, I knew something was wrong. He had his arm in a sling and was looking quite distressed.

'Are you alright, sir?' I asked.

'Yes, I am fine, Aleksandrov, but I have some bad news. Your old tank took a direct hit coming off the landing craft, I am very sorry but everyone inside was killed immediately. Lucky for you, I suppose, I am sorry about your chums, they were good men.'

I felt my knees buckle as he spoke. I had seen at first-hand what happens when the human body is torn apart by bullets and shrapnel.

'Yes Sir, thank you, Sir. Do you have any orders for me?'

'Yes, go and get some tea and then you are to join Lieutenant Scott, his driver took a shrapnel wound, you will be his driver.'

'Yes Sir,' and with that I walked out. It was quite surreal. I had spent the last year training with Harry, Albrecht, François and Ischmael. They were the closest thing to family I had and now they were gone. I then realized that it could have been me and was promptly sick. The adrenalin had got me through the day but suddenly fear crept up on me. I found a small space between a kitchen tent and a sand dune and knelt down and cried. After a few minutes, I recovered my composure and went and had some sweet tea. One thing that the British army was always good at was getting the food and drink set up as soon as possible. As I sat on a dune, I thought about how lucky I was to have changed tanks just the day before. I thought about Evie and wondered if I would ever see her again, how fragile life was and how we had to grab every moment and make the most of it.

There wasn't really too much time to rest, we were rushing to form a bridgehead so within an hour, I was back in a Cromwell tank under the command of Lieutenant D.S. Scott with two more Jews I knew from camp, Sasha, the radio operator, and Amos, the gunner, and a loader called Jimmy, a Glaswegian with a very thick accent. Our objective was the town of Bayeux. We had been told that this was a very strategic town as it was where the Germans were most likely to regroup and counter-attack.

The German resistance had been crushed on the beach and we did not encounter any Germans on the road as we rushed towards Bayeux. My new tank felt much more like home with pictures and scrawls all over the inside. The previous driver had taken a shrapnel wound when he left the tank thinking the Germans had all fled, it was from one of the big guns further behind the front line which is why I was transferred.

We were in the forefront of the column, looking for Germans which was pretty scary. As it happened, we were able to capture Bayeux within the day with very few casualties. It turned out that all the deceptions had worked and the Germans strength was in the wrong place. It was to take days before the Germans could regroup. Whilst in Bayeux, I was able to visit the Cathedral and see the famous tapestry. I was amazed at its length at 231 feet and wondered as to how it had survived the war. This was one of the bizarre things about the war; we were fighting in real places with real people and history all around us. One minute we might be trying to blow up a gun emplacement and very shortly afterwards we would be finding out if there was room in the local hotel and admiring the architecture."

"Are you saying that you actually saw the Bayeux Tapestry in the Cathedral?" said Roger incredulously.

"Yes. Are you so surprised? I was able to walk up to it and touch it," replied Leon. "As I said, as the invading army, we found some of the most incredible things."

"I went to see the tapestry on a French trip in year

9," said Claudia, "but it was behind glass." It was a coach trip.

"Perhaps you should have gone to see it in a twenty-five ton tank, they might have let YOU touch it then!" replied Leon.

They all laughed, except Roger.

"Go on Pepe, what happened after Bayeux?" asked Paul.

"Could I have a little drink, please Susan?" said Leon. "My throat is rather dry."

"Of course Pepe, water?" said Susan.

"Yes please, nice and cold from the tap, none of your fizzy bottled for me," replied Leon.

"I know," said Susan, calling from the kitchen, returning with a tumbler freshly filled from the tap.

"Thank you, that's better," said Leon, sipping on the liquid. He adjusted himself in his chair again and continued.

"We leaguered up at Sommervieu near Bayeux, regrouping and awaiting orders."

"What's leaguered?" asked Jonathan leaning forwards.

"It was a term we used in the army, I don't know if they still do," replied Pepe.

"It just means to regroup and refuel, getting ready for the next move, nothing more. A week later, on the 14th June, General De Gaulle Commander of the Free French Forces entered Bayeux and made a speech celebrating the real fighting France and restored National authority. This apparently caused some problems within the high command, as Roosevelt didn't want De Gaulle there. Roosevelt felt that De Gaulle wasn't representative of the French People. The American President refused to entrust him with

France's future and wanted instead to set up an Allied Military Government of Occupied Territories (AMGOT). The army came up with so many acronyms during the war. Political confusion was at its height and the fate of France would very much hang on the events of June 14th.

After his speech, De Gaulle immediately sang *Le Marseillaise*. He was received with rapturous applause and a month later Roosevelt was forced to recognize De Gaulle's authority over the liberated regions. De Gaulle knew how to play a crowd."

"How do you know that happened?" asked Roger again, somewhat derogatorily.

"Well Roger, I was very lucky. Whilst we were waiting in Sommervieu, I had borrowed a jeep and driven in to Bayeux with Sasha to look for some fresh bread and wine. Just as we arrived, De Gaulle was finishing his speech and we joined in with the singing. Captain Hillier, whom I hadn't seen since the landings, was part of the British contingency looking after De Gaulle. He knew that I spoke French. When he saw me in the crowd, he called me over and asked me to translate for him. I got to shake the future President's hand the day he returned to France."

"No way!" exclaimed Donna. "You met De Gaulle?! You never told us this before."

"I didn't think it was important, it was a different time. It wasn't part of my real life. My real life is here with you, my life in England. The war threw up circumstances that wouldn't normally happen.

After De Gaulle's speech, I managed to get away. Captain Hillier wanted me to continue with him at dinner with De Gaulle but I wanted to get back. Sasha and I returned to camp and were told to prepare to move out. We got everything packed up and went into formation.

Within no time at all we had run into the enemy and were heavily involved taking casualties. The Germans had regrouped and the element of surprise was gone, we were up against experienced troops who had armour, good leadership and were mobile. We had been given orders to cut the Caen-Bayeux highway and link up with the Americans who had broken out from Juno beach, but the going was tough. The Normandy countryside was not designed for tanks. The area was extremely heavily wooded and very suitable for the German defences, with their very accurate 88mm guns. We were facing German reinforcements including some Panzer divisions. We were always on the lookout for the infamous Tiger tanks as we knew our shells would just bounce off them.

Rommel had kept the Panzers back inland to be ready for a counter-attack. We were filled with fear and anticipation. By now I was getting to know my new crew really well. Lieutenant Scott was a very likeable chap. He had joined up early on in the war and had served everywhere. He was very experienced, as was Jimmy, our convivial Scot. He had served in the North Africa campaign. Apparently he had been promoted twice but demoted again as his relationship with alcohol was not a happy one. Sasha and Amos were in essence from the same school as me, part of the 'enemy aliens'. We all got on very well and knew the importance of working as a team. All of us in our twenties, facing the fiercest fighting machine the world had ever seen, we knew how much we had to rely on one another.

We fought at the Granville Crossroads and at Villers-Bocage, two very fierce battles. This was all part of some great plan to take the town of Caen which was considered to be strategically important. Eventually we linked up with the Americans and pushed into the town but were repelled by the Germans who had now dug themselves in. We knew this was not going to be a pushover. When we landed on the beaches, our deceptions had been so good that the Germans didn't know where we were going to land. Although the beaches were well defended and some of our troops, especially the Americans had a tough time of it, the Germans had always planned to regroup and counter-attack once they knew where our strengths were."

CHAPTER 7

The Greatest German Panzer Ace

"Unknown to us, amongst the Germans was one of their Panzer aces, Michael Wittman.

Wittman was aged only thirty but was already credited with the destruction of one hundred and thirty-eight tanks and one hundred and thirty-two anti-tank guns, along with an unknown number of other armoured vehicles, making him Germany's top scoring Panzer Ace.

Wittman was in command of a single Mark VI Tiger and, within a fifteen minute assault, had destroyed fourteen of our tanks as well as personnel carriers and anti-tank guns, he was a genius who seemed to have no fear, a lethal combination for us. I saw him knock out the first tank on a narrow road and then the last one, boxing in all the other vehicles which was a classic tactic. It left all the vehicles in between trapped and sitting ducks. He then manoeuvred up and down, taking each vehicle out as he went. Our own tanks hit him three or four times, but this was the first of the Mark VI Tigers we had seen and our shells were not affecting it at all. By the time our ant-tank guns had been brought up, he was gone. We had no option but to withdraw, the 13th of June was a bloody nose for the 8th Army. After his success, Hitler requested Wittman to become a tank instructor, however he refused and was killed on the

9th August. You have to give the man enormous credit, he could have avoided the war and just taught others but he wanted to carry on fighting.

Our command lost their appetite for this little village and, as was often the case, resorted to bombing it into rubble. We felt sorry for the innocent inhabitants who lived there who hadn't invited any of this. It reminded me of our Jewish plight, being persecuted for being in the wrong place at the wrong time. The village, or what was left of it, was finally liberated on the 4th August."

"Are you saying that you fought against Germany's greatest Panzer Ace?" asked Jonathan.

"I suppose I did, although really all we did was run away when we realised that the fight was lost. We couldn't get past all the vehicles that had been destroyed in the road, if we had tried and got stuck, we would have been blown up too, so I don't know if running away really counts as fighting but we were there for another day," said Leon jokingly.

"I celebrated my first wedding anniversary on the 18th June by sharing a couple of bottles of wine with Isaak after we had knocked out a couple of 88mm guns in the morning. I did not receive a letter about our wedding anniversary until two weeks later, such was the problem with the mail during the battles, but all said and done we did very well at the front line getting our post pretty regularly as the command knew this helped with morale. The wine was compliments of a French family who had cheered us after we destroyed the Germans guns; they gave us bread, wine and flowers. By now we had gained air superiority and had our first airfields in France. This gave us much more cover and made us feel a lot better. I seem to recall that evening Isaak and I got quite drunk.

The next day, despite having a hangover, we were ordered forwards to Briquessard where once again we fought fiercely against strong resistance from a small corps of *Waffen-SS*. Fortunately, they had no armour but they would not give up easily. Just when we thought we had them trapped, they managed to get away, as was often the case. The Germans were the experts at counter-attack; regroup and attack again. After two days of really tough fighting, the opposition had disappeared and on June 30th, we handed over our positions to tanks from the US 2nd Armoured Division and withdrew for a rest and a refit of our own tanks. Our Cromwell had taken a number of hits from machine guns and small arms but she had held up well, although Lieutenant Scott took a graze to his head when he put his head out of the turret. He was fine but it did remind me of Shorty.

The weather was awful and we could not find any indoor billets, we used great ingenuity to keep dry using ground sheets and gas capes and anything else that appeared vaguely waterproof as there were no tents or bivouacs available. Thus, for us, ended the first stages of the Battle of Normandy, sat wet in a field in the middle of the French countryside, hardly the reception we had been hoping for as the army of liberation but we were happy, especially as the mail had finally arrived.

I received sixteen letters in one go from Evie and spent the whole evening reading them over and over. I had thought about only opening one a day and saving them but couldn't wait, also in the back of my mind I thought about Albrecht and wondered if I would be next. We had all received a backlog of mail, so everyone was very quiet for a few hours. Evie's letters always filled me with such hope, even though she couldn't actually say that much. We were very limited as to what we could say and anything sensitive was censored. Just the smell of the letters was enough to lift me. The next day, I went off into the countryside and, using my French, was able to find a farm and was allowed use of their barn, at last we were out of the rain. Word started to spread about my French prowess. You have to remember, in those days, kids didn't even learn basic French at school, so I was very much in a minority but it was proving very advantageous.".

CHAPTER 8

The biggest tank battle in Europe at Caen

"We rested and re-fitted, awaiting our next orders. The City of Caen remained a key objective. Montgomery had hoped it would be captured on the first day of the landings but the Germans had quickly reinforced themselves and knew the strategic importance of the city themselves. We were to be part of 'Operation Goodwood', which some historians later called the largest tank battle that the British Army ever fought. Breaking out of the bridgehead had been painfully slow and Command was getting impatient. This impatience meant taking more risks with less planning, which meant things being even more dangerous; we all knew this.

As we had our supper, sitting around our tank, we all hoped that the command would just bomb Caen rather than sending us in. It was a terrible thought but to lose so many friends in that small French town of Villers-Bocage was frightening. We knew that the Germans were no pushover and that they would fight and constantly counter-attack, especially the Panzer Divisions.

The battle that ensued was very violent, with a lot of men lost and many tanks. It was almost a battle of attrition, where we had to knock out more of their tanks than they got of ours. The Germans had experienced this before at the Battle of Kursk outside

Moscow. That was the biggest tank battle of all time and some historians have said that that battle changed the course of the war. The Battle for Caen started on the 18th July. We had 62,000 men and 760 tanks. The objective was to write down the German Army's strength so that it was no longer effective. In other words, we had to keep going until the Germans had lost most of their tanks. This did not sound like a very good plan to us in our little tank and I can tell you we were very frightened, even if we did not tell one another. The battle actually started quite slowly and built up as the day went on. It was a very hard fought battle with substantial losses on both sides but the support of aerial bombardment meant it was over by the 20th. There was not a decisive breakthrough but fortunately the Germans did not have the resources to counter-attack.

We played our role in this battle, knocking out one German tank and capturing a number of German soldiers."

"How did you knock out the German Tank Pepe?" asked Jonathan.

"It wasn't anything special. We were attacking the east of the city and approaching in a column when we came under fire. We rushed forwards into the outskirts and were momentarily stopped behind a building waiting for orders when we saw a Panzer come out from behind another building fifty yards away. We had a clear broadside shot and hit it first time, its tracks coming off. As it tried to turn to return fire we hit it again. We saw the lids pop open and the tank crew came out and immediately surrendered with their hands up in the air, not surprising as our machine gun was trained on them. I think this panicked half a dozen German soldiers who had been supporting the tank and they immediately threw down their weapons. A few others quickly retreated and disappeared in the rubble. This was very good for us as we now had eleven prisoners that we had to secure and retire to the rear which took us out of the battle for a little while.

The sheer ferocity of the fighting meant that the Germans considered the joint British and Canadian armies to be their greatest threat and so they reduced their forces against the Americans, who now only faced one and a half Panzer divisions whilst the British and Canadians faced six and a half. Once the American First Army broke through the German defences in 'Operation Cobra' on the 25th July there weren't sufficient reserves because they had all been moved against us, leaving the Americans to break out. Perhaps this battle was more important than has been recorded, it is certainly not one of those that they make films about but it probably did change the course of the war."

"That's amazing," said Jonathan. "I had never even heard of it, and you were there!"

"I only played a small part, there were a lot of us there, you know," replied Leon.

"Many Germans remained in the Normandy area and were always a threat. A few days after the Battle of Caen, Field Marshall Montgomery was touring the troops and came to see us to tell us how well we had all done. We all knew that Monty wanted to be the first to Berlin and was after all the glory. The 8th Army were pleased to follow because Monty had won the North Africa Campaign (single-handedly, he would have many believe) but I worried that he might try and do things that were too risky, to further his career, and we were the cannon fodder."

CHAPTER 9

Escaping Death at the Falaise Gap

"On the 12th August, Montgomery in his usual search for glory saw an opportunity to capture two whole German Armies, the 5th and 7th Panzers. The battle raged for nine days but eventually they were both trapped in an engagement called the Falaise Gap. This was the decisive manoeuvre in the west that led the way open to Paris which was captured on the 23rd August.

During these engagements came my most difficult time in the war.

I was in the Forêt de Montfort, south east of Le Havre, as part of the force involved in the Falaise Gap. We were trying to close the gap and stop the Germans escaping. The Germans knew that if we closed the loop, they would be captured or killed and these were Panzer divisions so they were going to fight to the death if necessary. It seemed that being captured was not an option for the more fanatical amongst them.

I was in my fourth tank of the campaign, the previous one having been abandoned due to mechanical failure and subsequently dispatched by enemy artillery. Reliability was a continual problem with our tanks; I suppose they had been rushed both in design and manufacture to get them to the front

line and were being replaced at a rate of knots to keep
the pressure on the retreating Germans. The troop I
was in consisted of three tanks, each manned by five
men. We were leading forward action. We knew that
our chances in such action were 50/50, but in these
circumstances a lot lower. On this occasion we came
across a very well camouflaged German anti-tank
position which had no difficulty in targeting our two
tanks, the third having broken down a few hundred
yards behind us.

Both our tanks were hit immediately by the very
accurate 88mm guns, which cut through the steel
without any difficulty entering in through the front
and exiting out of the back of the tank. My tank
Commander Lieutenant D.S. Scott was killed
instantly. The remaining nine of us jumped out and
abandoned our tanks and ran as fast as we could as
the fuel and ammunition were about to explode. As
soon as we were out, the supporting German machine
gun fire started. We ran, trying to dodge the bullets.
Fortunately there was a corn field nearby. I ran as fast
as I could and literally dived into the cover. I began
crawling through the furrows, through the corn
stubble which was quite low as it had been harvested
recently, trying to get back to our units which were a
thousand yards from this point. I realized that I was
completely on my own; none of my crew were with
me.

The Germans were good with the machine guns,
killing four and, as I later found out, capturing the
other four. Of the ten men in the two tanks, I was the
only one that managed to reach a British Observation
Tank. I began to think that Jehovah was really looking
over me as one of Zion's children. Lieutenant Scott

and Amos both died that day. Sasha and Jimmy were taken off to a prisoner of war camp."

I kept going through the corn field, keeping as low as possible. I heard machine gun fire and thought that they were probably just firing haphazardly. After a few minutes, the gunfire stopped but I didn't look back, I was unarmed and there was nothing I could do. I knew that none of the others had made it into the relative safety of the corn field. Through the field, across a ditch and then across another field, I could see the shape of some of our vehicles and knew that I had made it back to our own lines. I stood up but when I approached one of our tanks I was told to put my hands up. My shirt was badly torn and very bloody as was my face from crawling through the stubble, the crew of the tank didn't know if I was British or German. I shouted out to them and managed to persuade them to radio back to my unit to verify who I was and to tell them that I had survived."

"Wow!" said Paul. "That's amazing, so you were the only one of the fifteen to escape?"

"Yes," said Leon. "Unfortunately the tank that broke down was hit by the 88mm and burst into flames, the crew were all burned alive inside."

"What happened to Sasha and Jimmy?" asked Olivia.

"Sasha spent the next ten months in a prisoner of war camp near Berlin. He was liberated in March of 1945. He and I remained good friends the rest of our lives, although he married a German girl and settled in Germany after the war," replied Leon.

"And… Jimmy?" asked Olivia again, this time nervously.

"Poor Jimmy," said Leon. "Only a week after arriving at a prisoner of war camp, he tried to escape. He jumped into a washing basket in the back of a lorry but was found when the lorry was stopped on the outside of the camp."

"What happened to him?" asked Jonathan

"They shot him there and then. He was still within sight of the barracks. Sasha saw it happen. They got him out of the basket, made him kneel down and shot him through the back of the head. I didn't find this out until a year later when I caught up with Sasha in Berlin." Leon took another sip of water and once again wiped a tear from his eye. "The war was turning against the Germans and their behaviour becoming more erratic. The shooting of escaping prisoners became more commonplace as a deterrent."

Anita and Hannah gasped almost simultaneously.

"You mean they just shot him in cold blood," said Paul." But what about the Geneva Convention, weren't there rules about how prisoners were to be treated?"

Hannah started to sob. Her father, Anthony, moved across to hug her.

"I am sorry, Hannah, I didn't mean to upset you," said Leon. "Perhaps I should stop. I knew it was not a good idea to tell you these things, they are better left in the past."

"No Pepe! I want to hear, I will be fine," she said. "It was just such a shock when you said it. I will be fine now. I don't know why that was such a surprise after the other things you talked about, please carry on."

"Are you sure? I don't want to upset anybody, I suppose this is why I have never talked about it. It was something that I wanted to leave behind, I don't really know why I am telling you all this now," said Leon, distraught that he had made his grand-daughter so upset. She wasn't the only one. Donna and Susan were both struggling to hold back the tears, as were Claudia and Benjamin.

"Perhaps it's time for a break," said Paul. "Tea anyone?" Hands were raised and orders taken.

"Give me a hand, Roger, will you?"

"Sure," came the reply.

In the kitchen, Paul beavered away with the kettle whilst Roger assembled the mugs on the tray.

"What do you think of the old man's story then?" asked Roger.

"It's quite amazing really. I just can't understand why he has never spoken about any of it before," replied Paul.

"You don't really think it can all be true, do you?" said Roger. "It's like something out of Forrest Gump. Meeting De Gaulle, everyone getting killed or captured but him... twice! It all seems a bit unbelievable," said Roger, laying out the sugar pot and spoons.

"What reason would he have for making it up and why now?" It wasn't difficult to tell that Paul was irritated by Roger's insinuation.

"Maybe he is just getting confused, after all, he is a very old man, that's all I am saying," replied Roger.

"Roger, I have known Leon for all the years I have known Jane, which is close on twenty-five. I cannot imagine for one minute that he would make it up or get so confused as to whether all of his friends were blown to bits, so just leave it, ok!" Paul's voice raised as he finished his sentence.

"Everything all right out there?" called Anthony from the lounge.

"Fine, fine, Roger thinks Arsenal will beat Chelsea on Boxing Day, it made me a bit excited," replied Paul.

"For once, I think I might agree with Roger," called Anthony. "Is that tea ready yet? We are all parched."

"Coming," said Paul.

"Just leave it Roger, not a word, ok?" said Paul.

"I was just asking the question, that's all. It does seem pretty unbelievable," replied Roger.

Back in the lounge, the girls started distributing the mugs of tea and the chocolate biscuits.

"Will you go on, Pepe?" asked Benjamin.

"Only if you are all ok and your parents say it is alright, I don't want to upset anyone, especially as it is Christmas."

"Please go on, Pepe, I still can't believe you have never spoken about any of this before," said Donna.

"OK, but if anyone gets upset I will stop. Now, where was I?" said Leon.

"You had just been blown up and crawled back to base through the fields," said Hannah.

"That's right, and there I was standing there with all of my uniform shredded and covered in blood. Once I had it verified that I was who I said I was, they sent a small armoured car to pick me up and take me back to my regiment, where it was established, once the blood was washed off, that I wasn't wounded. They took my clothes off and were about to throw them away when I remembered that I had my photos of Evie in the pocket. They were a bit

102

crumpled after my exertions but were the most precious thing I had at that time. I had now mislaid another crew and was beginning to wonder if I was jinxed."

CHAPTER 10

A Dingo and George Formby on The Ukulele

"I was temporarily put on a two man armoured car called a Dingo, which could go at the same speed backwards as it could forwards. I suppose the idea was to prevent me suffering too much from shock, so they wanted to keep me busy. There were no tanks for me to go to as we had lost so many fighting over the previous two weeks and were waiting for new ones to arrive.

A couple of days later, George Formby arrived to entertain the troops. We were all stood around while George sat on a tank turret and played *My Little Ukulele*, *Blackpool Rock* and *When I'm Cleaning Windows*. The whole thing was quite surreal. We had been fighting one of the bloodiest military campaigns and here was Gorge Formby playing his ukulele.

As our numbers had been depleted by the fighting, we were reinforced by a squadron from the Northamptonshire Yeomanry. This was often the case that forces were merged to re-build fighting strength. The same thing was happening with the Germans. I received letters from Evie that kept my strength up. A week might go past when nothing arrived and then suddenly eight letters would come at once and my heart would leap. Because there was always a big time delay between sending my letters and hearing back that they had been received, everything seemed to be out of time. Of course, I couldn't say where we were or what we were doing and Evie couldn't say what was happening in Britain either as all mail was being checked, there was always the fear that the post bags would fall into enemy hands and give away positions or secrets. Everyone had their own secret language with their loved ones, using past events as a sort of code so we were able to get a little bit past the censors but we were all aware of the importance of the advance and so were very careful about what we said.

The Battle of the Falaise Gap had been brutal. As the Germans were trapped, the Allies bombarded them with artillery and from the air. There were burning vehicles and bodies everywhere and hundreds of dead horses, which were still being used to tow artillery by the Germans. After the German retreat we were able to advance very quickly and relatively unopposed. The Germans we did come across tended to surrender rather than fight. We continued to push through France heading towards the Seine, a distance of about seventy-five miles across the Compagne of Picardy. We had hoped that the Germans might just give up but we found out that that wasn't the case."

CHAPTER 11

Advancing through France

"Although the Germans were in full retreat, the countryside still gave them the opportunity to mount a defence. Here, the landscape is not like the *bocage* to the west of Caen but the rivers were still wide and possible to defend. We were a key part of the general advance supporting the 11th Hussars. The Luftwaffe was still active at night but had long lost air superiority so barely attacked during the day as they were a real problem for tanks so we were glad to see the back of them. We crossed the River Vie and captured the town of Livarot. We were greeted by the townsfolk waving flowers and bottles of wine. My mates asked me to translate for them, hoping to win the favours of the French girls who had come to greet us, but as always I had my commanding officer on my shoulder asking about atrocities. I tried to help my pals when I could, it would have been rude not to, but because of my languages I was being used more and more often as a translator.

The bridge over the Vie was strengthened by the engineers to allow the 22nd Armoured Brigade to cross that afternoon and we were soon advancing on the road to Lisieux towards the River Touques. We were pressing quite hard now trying to keep the Germans on the run not allowing them to re-group and counter-attack. Because of the pressure we were applying the Germans weren't getting the chance to blow all the bridges as part of their retreat. We found a bridge intact and on the 21st August the advance continued. We came across small groups of German troops and tanks periodically, but it was clear that these were just independent groups fighting a rear-guard action. The biggest danger was from mines and booby-traps although we were always fearful when we saw a Tiger tank, usually from the remnants of the 12th SS Panzer Division. It would have been nice to think that the Germans were running out of tanks, but production figures that came out after the war showed that tank production was at its highest in 1944 at 19,000 or fifty-three tanks a day coming off the production lines many of which were the new Tigers or the Panzer IV.

Part of our job was to destroy the tanks faster than they could make them. Even though we were making good progress towards Germany, and the RAF and the USA were bombing the factories in Germany, the German war machine still produced 4,400 tanks in the last few months of the war in 1945. Aircraft production also peaked in 1944 at 35,000 aircraft, including 5,500 ground attack aircraft and 13,000 Messerschmitt 109s, although towards the end of the war the Luftwaffe had run out of pilots. Even in the first few months of 1945, 7,000 planes rolled off the production line. It was the German war machine's ability to produce such vast quantities of weapons that contributed to the war lasting as long as it did," said Leon.

"How do you know all this?" asked Roger accusingly.

"I will tell you that later at the end of my little

story," replied Leon knowingly.

"Where was I, ah yes, the town of Lisieux. It was very well defended but did eventually surrender after a couple of days fighting. Our supply lines were by now functioning very well so we always had superiority in armour during this period. With little rest we chased ten miles down the main Route National to the River Risle waved on by groups of cheering Frenchmen. Unfortunately when we got to the river, all the bridges had been blown up, but after advancing twenty-six miles in two days, the Division was on top form. Eager to press on we searched along the river and found a bridge intact near Montfort meaning the whole Division could cross. We laid up for twenty-four hours to rest and re-fit. This gave me the chance to re-read my letters from Evie and to write a new letter. We were very fortunate that the grateful French gave us food and wine. The advance had been so swift that the Germans did not have time to plunder or destroy in their retreat. For the first time in weeks, I slept. There was no sound of gunfire, no bombs dropping. There was relative peace. It had only been eleven weeks since we landed in France, but so much had happened since then, it felt like a lifetime.

The French were extremely grateful that we had arrived and relieved that the Germans had just retreated through them quickly without destroying their homes on the way.

After the re-fit, for the next three days we pushed on across rolling wooded countryside, between the Risle and the Seine, taking so many prisoners during short actions against small pockets of German troops. These small groups were still very dangerous but they had no support and were generally quickly overcome. We pushed on continuously and by the evening of the 28th August, we reached the Seine by the Forêt de Bretonne. The last few weeks had been tough and we had suffered, there is no question about that. We had taken losses and had all been affected by the fighting but we had come through and were in fighting form again. I was in a new tank, which had arrived directly from the port with no delivery mileage, as the allies now had control of the railways. I spent a couple of days putting her through her paces as I had learned the hard way the importance of reliability and speed. I was assigned a new crew, which was now my fourth. Like most other divisions, my new crew was cannibalised from other outfits. My new commanding officer was Roger Haimes, a captain, Charlie Brooker, gunner, Terry Lowndes, loader, and Billy Jackson on radio.

For the first time, I, as an 'enemy alien' and a Jew, was in the minority but by now I was an experienced driver and in demand and news of my ability to find goodies from the French using my languages had spread, so I was welcomed with open arms, especially as I was able to lay on a welcoming feast for my new crew of wine, cheese, some ham and a bottle of Cognac. We spent a few days getting to know one another whilst testing our new tank. Our paths had actually crossed at West Toft's, although we didn't really know one another. We worked out we were there at the same time, Charlie Brooker, Billy Jackson and myself. They took great pleasure in reminding me how I drove the first tank that almost drowned in England. Sadly, it turned out that Billy and Harry Fathers, my commanding officer, were related, he also found out upon landing that my first tank crew had taken a direct hit, I think this shared pain made us very close from that day onwards.

Anyway, back to the war. The original German Army we had been facing in Normandy had been made up of ten Panzer Divisions and fourteen German infantry divisions. This had been reduced to only one hundred and fifteen tanks and about sixty five thousand men who had escaped, to try and re-group across the Seine. They were by now so depleted with many of their best soldiers killed or captured. So much was happening so quickly as the allies were advancing pretty fast and the Germans were in disarray. You have to remember that they were fighting on three fronts really. Everyone always talks about the Russian Front and the Western Front but of course there was a sizeable battle going on in Italy which was taking up a lot of German resources. By the 25th of August the Free French, under General Le Clerc, had re-captured Paris. When we heard, we were elated and any French we met were besides themselves, the wine and flowers just kept coming, it was like a continual party and by the 30th, Patton's Americans were in Sedan and Verdun. We still felt as though the war would be over by Christmas, such was the speed of our advances. I was dreaming of Christmas with Evie and my family in Islington, I imagined a tree and a scene just like this one with my family around me but we had a long way to go.

Our tank was always one of the advanced vehicles because our commanding officer had discovered that I could speak French and German. My language skills were not quite as popular now with the rest of my tank crew, as they knew that this always put us in more danger. Every time we came across the local French people, I was pushed to the front to tell them that we were here to liberate them. That had its own risks, as quite often the retreating Germans left booby traps or worse still, snipers to pick off allied officers.

I had to ask if there were any Germans nearby or hiding. We started to hear stories of atrocities of some villagers being shot as reprisals for the resurgent French resistance. These were usually committed by the *Waffen-SS*. We took notes of names and descriptions of the perpetrators, not really knowing what we should do with them. This became more and more common as we moved from Vichy France to the German controlled areas, we were instructed to gather as much information as we could and there was already talk of war crime trials. It seemed like an eternity since I was learning my French in Lausanne and using it in prison in Nevers but it continued to improve, although the accent was always a little unusual. Unfortunately, my vocabulary had to improve to accommodate some dreadful words. Nobody should need to learn immolation in another language."

"What's immolation?" asked Claudia.

Everyone was silent.

"Are you sure you want to know?" replied Leon.

"I think so," said Claudia.

"It's when someone is set alight," said Leon gravely.

"How can you set someone alight? If you put a match to them, they wouldn't burn," replied Claudia naively.

"They would if you poured petrol all over them first," replied Pepe.

There was a cold silence in the room. Leon shuffled in his chair, pulling the blanket across his knees and continued.

We were advancing, supporting the First Canadian army. As we moved up through France, my unit came across an abandoned site for the 'doodlebugs' that had been used as a launch site."

"I know all about the doodlebugs, the V1s and the V2s," said Benjamin. "I saw a programme on them, Spitfires used to tilt the wings of the V1s to push them off course but the V2s were much faster, the first inter-continental ballistic missiles, they say that most modern day missiles are a variation of the V2. You got to see the V2s, Pepe?"

"Actually Benjamin, I didn't get to see them at all. We had been rushed up to these sites as Hitler had ordered the use of more and more of his 'Vengeance Weapons' and they had been devastating. From the week after the D-Day landings until the 1st of September almost 9,000 flying bombs were catapulted from the north of France towards London. Only 2,300 made it to the target but they caused immense destruction with over 6,000 people killed, mainly in the East End. After the war, Evie told me that she had been in London during that time and had rushed to the bomb shelters as the flying bombs came over. She told me that everyone was terrified when the engines cut out and the bombs started falling. It was hard for Londoners to imagine that the war was coming to an end when these new weapons were being used. The push through France was hurried along to stop these rocket bases, although none of us knew this at the time. We were just focused on what was happening around us and didn't realize the impact of these bombs, don't forget we didn't have television or the internet and most of the news was censored. When we arrived at the rocket base, everyone had left, and in a hurry, there was still food and personal effects lying around so it was clear that the Germans kept launching until the very last minute although there were no rockets left when we arrived. By then, they had worked out how to keep them mobile," said Leon.

"Wow, wait until I tell me friends at school that my grandfather stopped the doodlebugs! That is sick," said Benjamin.

"I don't think that's even true!" said Pepe. "When we arrived everything had gone, they knew we were coming and had withdrawn behind their own lines, I doubt if we even stopped them firing the bombs, they were still in range for a little while. Can you pass me some water, please, Susan?" asked Leon.

"Of course, Pepe." His daughter passed him his glass, from which he took a few sips, she topped it up from the jug and Leon continued.

CHAPTER 12

Into Belgium

"We crossed the border into Belgium. Some villages were empty of the enemy when we got to them; others had to be fought for. Snipers were the biggest fear but, as I said, by then I had another tank wrapped around me. As the driver, I would keep my little observation hole closed when we entered these villages as it was becoming common for the sniper to try and take out the driver of the lead vehicle, clogging up the road, leaving the rest of the convoy open to attack by the deadly accurate 88mm gun that the Germans were using to great effect in their retreat. I became quite adept at driving only able to see through a hole little bigger than a matchbox. Large parts of western Belgium were quickly liberated as the Germans concentrated their defences in certain key areas. There were still some significant battles to be fought but Brussels had already been liberated.

Wherever we went in Belgium, we were showered with gifts from the grateful Belgian people. These were people who had been living in the shadow of the Nazis for five long years. As we spoke to them, we heard about more and more atrocities and it became clear that it was the Jews, or anyone who had helped them, who were bearing the brunt of their brutality. Although I didn't speak Flemish, many people from Belgium also spoke French and even German. I was translating so I was hearing everything first. It is a terrible thing to say, but after a while you become numb to what you hear. I found myself translating, word for word, some appalling things, just concentrating on getting the language correct rather than what I was actually saying. By now the horror of it all was becoming apparent and all too common.

We hadn't really had a big battle since the Falaise Gap but now we were ordered to take the Ghent Canal. The Germans had been withdrawing steadily, preparing to make a stand at key locations, and this was one of them. The ever increasing allied army in Europe needed supplying and it needed a deep water port. The Germans knew this, which is why Antwerp and the waters leading up to it were so well defended. Here the Germans couldn't be bombed into submission; it had to be taken on the ground.

The Operation started on the 31st of August but on the 4th September our Division was ordered to strike directly for Ghent. We were using so much fuel that it was impossible to keep the whole force mobile as we were by now so far ahead of headquarters and often operating beyond the maps that we had. A smaller force was formed called 'The Ghent Force', which raced along for fifty miles being covered in flowers, grapes and wine as it went by grateful locals. It was impossible to stop, otherwise we would have been smothered. At Ghent, one of the many strange events of the war occurred. The German garrison had over a thousand men supported by 88mm guns, quite a formidable force but fortunately they were prepared to surrender as they knew they couldn't hold out for ever. The German General Daser approached our Lt Colonel Holliman. The General said that he was prepared to surrender but only to a British Officer of equivalent rank. Holliman tried to pass himself off but one of his men accidentally called him 'Colonel', so Brigadier Mackeson came forward and persuaded General Daser that he was almost a General. Daser duly surrendered, sparing Ghent from almost certain destruction even though by then Daser had received orders to fight on.

The next day the city was entered and we parked our tanks outside the Town Hall. We spent the next three days clearing pockets of resistance, which was very hazardous as there were many snipers and we were still way ahead of the rest of the British forces. We found so much German booty here. It was all meant to be handed in but we kept wine, sausage, cognac and even a bottle of champagne, which we shared amongst our crew. It was the first time that Billy, Terry or Charlie had ever had champagne. We were all quite tiddly that night.

We now entered a period of cat and mouse. To the south of Ghent was the German 15th Army led by General Von Zangen, but unknown to us there was the build-up of force for Operation Market Garden, you may have seen the film with Sean Connery, Michael Caine and any other big star that Hollywood could get into a uniform. I saw it; it glamorised the war, I didn't like it. This was Montgomery's idea to finish the war by Christmas or, as we called it, the chance to be the first allied General to Berlin. We didn't do very much for the next few weeks, just mopping up small pockets of resistance. We then heard about the great airborne assault. We were hearing snippets of news but then we found out on the 25th of September that it hadn't been a success. So many of our brave troops died on that venture, I can tell you that the average soldier was not very pleased with Montgomery. Our own captain, Haimes, was very upset, he really cared about our welfare and didn't like the gung-ho approach of some of the generals."

CHAPTER 13

Holland beckons

"A couple of days later we moved into Holland, taking up positions at Sint Oedenrode which had been liberated by the American 101st Airborne a week earlier as part of Operation Market Garden. From there, we moved on to the Rhine, the last great obstacle before entering Germany. We fought hard on the way to St Pol, where we met fierce resistance as was becoming the case now as we closed in on Germany. As you can imagine, it was one thing for the Germans to be fighting in France or Belgium but another thing to be defending their homeland.

During October, the Division held the line west of the town of 's-Hertogenbosch and then gradually moved into positions south and east of the River Maas. The front here was quite wide and we were taking a steady stream of casualties and weren't really getting the reinforcements as new recruits weren't being trained fast enough. Our Commanders thought it best to re-distribute the experienced fighters in different roles.

Our division came across a German supply depot in the town of Oss. The Germans had been retreating so fast that they had left the majority of the contents behind. There was bacon, cheese, butter - food no one had seen for ages. I was immediately brought up to the front to speak to the Dutchman in charge.

Although I didn't speak Dutch, we understood each other pretty well with a little bit of sign language. Once again our crew ate very well and I was Mr Popular!"

"Pepe, it sounds as though all you thought about was your stomach!" said Jonathan.

"Actually, all I thought about was your grandmother, but food kept us going. Our rations were really pretty poor, unlike the Americans, who seemed to have everything. We probably could have had as much food as we wanted, we were the victors and this part of the countryside had been relatively unaffected by the war before we came through, but we didn't think it was right to take what we wanted, we were very happy to relieve the Germans of anything they had stolen or plundered but we couldn't do that to the French, the Belgians or the Dutch. It was feast or famine really, one day we might find some little treasure trove of German plunder and then it was back to basic rations. We had no complaints, at that time the Dutch were starving because of German blockades, quite often we would redistribute the food that we found.

We had enjoyed a few days rest and the chance to enjoy the German booty we had found but then at the end of October we were ordered to advance on Emelhuen about thirty miles away. Between us and our objective was thickly wooded country, leading on to polder country which is large fields surrounded by dykes. Much like the *bocage* in Normandy it was not ideal for tanks, We knew we would be very susceptible to ambush as there was little room to manoeuvre or turn around. It was the perfect landscape for defence and probably the worst for attack and the Germans that remained since the D-Day landings were by now very experienced and knew our weaknesses.

We were not very happy in our tank, this was dangerous and I recalled my experience when I narrowly escaped across the fields. I had told my new crew and friends about what had happened and wished I had kept it to myself. We advanced with flail and the new Crocodile flame throwing Churchill tanks in the lead. These were fearsome weapons that had joined us since Normandy. They would tow a tank of petroleum jelly and fire a flame one hundred yards into the distance. The jelly would stick to anything and was a frightening weapon. One of the most terrifying things about war is our ability as humans to design ever more destructive weapons. New weapons were arriving at the front with regularity, unfortunately on both sides.

The Germans were dug-in in village strongpoints manned by infantry and artillery, surrounded by mines. They adopted all sorts of tactics like sending out someone from the village with a white flag indicating surrender. We would enter the town or village only to discover an 88mm gun concealed that would take out our first tank and open fire on our infantry. They were quickly overcome because they were so well concealed they had no room to escape. They should have been taken prisoner but our troops were so disgusted by this cowardly tactic they were often shot on the spot. They were organised by the fanatical *SS* who threatened to kill their own civilians if they didn't agree. It made it very hard entering any village as we were always wary. I quickly learnt enough Dutch to tell the citizens to stay in their homes and not to approach us to avoid unnecessary casualties. We crossed the river and fought a number of battles before pressing on towards Dongan, where we received a warm welcome from the Dutch and an even warmer one from a group of Germans with tank and artillery support and this is the way it was, every day was a struggle against fierce German resistance and we expected nothing less. We lost over twenty tanks just clearing these small towns and villages and a lot of good men, it was heart-breaking.

By now we knew the rest of the war was not going to be a pushover. The Germans were not going to capitulate and surrender *en masse* as we had hoped. We were also hearing about the fighting that was going on at the Eastern Front, we heard that the fighting there was even more ferocious and that the Russians were suffering huge casualties. We had heard the stories of the atrocities that the Germans had done to the poor Russian people, so it was no surprise that it was happening the other way round. In some respects, this was good news for us as the Eastern Front was keeping some of the best German units occupied, I can't imagine what it would have been like if we had been fighting the whole of the German army.

The start of November saw little contact with the enemy and the troops enjoyed being billeted in warm Dutch houses, when not on guard or overhauling the tanks and equipment, I took this opportunity to learn a little Dutch with a family I was billeted with. He was a teacher who spoke some English. We taught each other during those days. It was good to be doing something normal. I spent a lot of the time playing cards with the rest of the crew, with Terry taking most of our cigarettes off us."

"But Pepe, you don't smoke! You always said you hated smoking," exclaimed Susan.

"I know, I know, but in the war everyone smoked, especially the soldiers fighting, it calmed the nerves and alleviated the boredom, it was also a currency, it seemed like the most natural thing in the world, you have to remember that in those days we didn't know it was bad for you, anyway, I don't suppose that would have made any difference, every day we were facing death, I don't think we would have worried about cancer or anything like that.

We enjoyed this little break, the Allied Armies, American, Canadian and British, had been on the move for four months so with France, Belgium and most of southern Holland free of Germans, there was time for a short pause, before the final big push into Germany.

On 10th November, we took up fresh positions along the River Maas. Everything was soaking wet, the grass was turning to mud wherever we drove or marched and everywhere was full of mines which made advancing painfully slow. The weather was absolutely miserable; we were more worried about the wet and the cold than the Germans! We were now wearing new multi-zipped winter clothing, which we affectionately called 'zoot-suits' but how we needed them. We were very pleased for this new innovation, they were sort of quilted and much warmer than our normal battle dress. Every little battle was a costly one now. Even though we had air superiority and were better equipped than the Germans, they kept fighting on. Our battalion was becoming ever more depleted by battle casualties.

You may find this hard to believe with the war at

such a crucial stage, bearing in mind a lot of our army had been fighting for years and were very experienced, but there was something called the 'Python' orders. All men who had served overseas for five years could be returned to the UK. This depleted us of a lot of very experienced fighting men who were replaced with more inexperienced recruits, not something we wanted as the fighting was getting fiercer.

On 7th December, we moved east across the Maas to support a new front. On the 16th of December, the very famous German counter offensive in the Ardennes started - 'The Battle of the Bulge' - but our Division was not involved. This explained why it had been so quiet for the previous month, with very few counter-attacks, the Germans had been building strength for what turned out to be their last throw of the dice. Films were made about this as well. Fortunately for us, the Germans lost a lot of the new Tiger tanks in that campaign, most of them just ran out of fuel and were abandoned, good news for us as we were still struggling to dent them with our shells!

As winter was approaching we painted our Cromwell tanks white for camouflage against the snow that was now falling. With rumours of Germans dressing up as Americans coming out of the Ardennes, a few jeep loads of real Americans were arrested as a precaution at this time. We thought this was very funny but they did not! Of all the things you may have read or seen about the war, something is rarely talked about, the cold of that winter of 1944, one of the coldest ever recorded in Europe with temperatures as low as -20 Celsius.

The weather was bitterly cold and we came up

with all sorts of ideas to keep the tanks functional and ourselves warm. We left lamps burning in the tank turrets all night and the engines of all vehicles had to run every two hours to prevent them freezing up so we had to create a rota to be able to do this which interrupted everybody's sleep, if you could sleep that was such was the cold. Even the oil on the machine guns had to be removed as it froze too. I was now in a recently acquired Sherman Firefly with a seventeen pounder gun, but even with the engine running it was like sitting in an ice box surrounded by all that cold metal. I had so many clothes on, I could barely move! Frostbite was the real enemy at this time, there was little chance of an attack as the Germans had the same problems we did. The weather was so poor there was no flying going, so no air support, so we just sat put, trying not to freeze, which was not easy.

The division arranged a Christmas concert party for us, which went off well. I went with a few of the other guys from our division and had a restful couple of days, I was able to find a bed and a warm shower and get all of my clothes washed, such simple pleasures, and I remember the joy of sitting at a table and enjoying some wine in a glass for a change in a little restaurant but before I knew it, I had returned back to my regiment. The Division enjoyed what it could of what was to be the last Christmas of the war, listening to the King's Speech and a broadcast from Montgomery, although that was spoilt by a German attack on Christmas night, we lost some vehicles and tanks. You would have thought the Germans would take one day off from the war!"

"That seems really mean," said Jonathan, "What about all those stories of the Germans and the British playing football on Christmas Day?"

"That was in the First World War, when the two armies were only fifty yards apart and could shout out and talk to each other, this was very different with really fast attacks with planes and vehicles.

What I haven't told you about was where we were staying at this time. When the army arrives anywhere, the first thing we do is find some billets," said Leon.

"What are billets?" asked Claudia. "Like dormitories?"

"Not exactly," replied Leon.

As the conquering army we could commandeer any building we wanted at the commanding officer's discretion. Different divisions or battalions had different ideas of what was and wasn't acceptable. If we found a house where the occupants were known Nazi sympathizers then we might take it over completely and even eat their food, but Captain Haimes was a real gentleman and had a policy not to take anything from those who had been persecuted by the Germans. Normally commanding officers would get superior lodgings but Captain Haimes always wanted to be with his men.

He asked me to seek out some accommodation. Because of the weather, we knew we might be staying there some time. I came across a small farm and introduced myself to the owner, who was very wary. If you recall, I had learned some Dutch from a previous billet which made him a little more comfortable but he lived there with his wife and daughter, who was probably about twenty years old and very pretty. I understood why he was concerned. He, like us, would have heard about all the rapes that were happening during the German retreats and also with the advancing armies."

"What do you mean the rapes?" asked Hannah.

"Sweet Hannah, this was war. You have to understand that people do terrible things they wouldn't normally do in peacetime. Many of the soldiers on both sides were just ordinary people before the war, teachers, doctors, bus drivers, but the war makes people think differently and do terrible things. When someone thinks all is lost, they lose control of themselves and do things they would never consider normally. Men who have been away for a long time can resort to such awful things. One man sees another do these things and after a while it becomes normal. The women had a terrible time at the end of the war, it was lawless and everyone was in terrible danger. The Allies were meant to be better behaved but there are always bad apples."

CHAPTER 14

Love in The Polders

"I introduced myself to the owner of the farm, who introduced himself as Arend Jansen. My Dutch was pretty basic but I was able to make him understand that we needed to use his home for a little while. Naturally, he was quite fearful and reluctant. He called out and his wife appeared, he introduced her as Greet and then his son, Ewoud, and finally his daughter, Esme."

"What! Aunt Esme?" shrieked Jane.

"Yes, that's right," said Pepe. "But of course, she wasn't your real aunt, that is just what we all called her."

"So Uncle Billy was Billy Jackson from your tank crew?" added Donna.

"Yes, that is so," replied Pepe.

"I don't understand. Why did you never tell us this? We knew Aunt Esme was Dutch but you never said you met during the war or that Billy was with you, none of you ever mentioned it," said Donna.

"After the war, everyone just wanted to move on; we didn't want to keep remembering it. By now though, you will have gathered that Billy and Esme fell in love. We were billeted with the Jansen's for almost three weeks, during which time they got to know one another. As soon as the war was over, Billy returned to the Jansen's farm where he stayed for the next fifteen years. Ewoud didn't want to continue with the farm once his father had passed away so Esme and Billy came to live in England, which is how you all know them." Pepe held his hands open as if to help the explanation.

"That's just amazing," said Susan. "We knew you two got on so well but that is just incredible."

"I don't know, not so incredible, two young people meet, they fall in love then spend the rest of their lives together, is it that surprising?" said Leon.

"Yes, but under those circumstances, the war and everything," said Susan.

"Many loves flourished during that time. Once I left for Europe, I didn't get to see your mother for over a year and until then, we hardly knew each other really, these were different times, every moment was precious, that's just how it was.

Anyway, we stayed at the Jansen's for over three weeks. It was bitterly cold but Captain Haimes refused to move the Jansen's out of their house. The five of us made a makeshift home in the cattle barns. It was a bit smelly and noisy but the warmth from the animals helped keep the building warm. We commandeered some food and shared our rations and ate almost every meal with the Jansens like one big happy family.

Billy quickly learned Dutch, as he now had good reason to, and even Charlie picked up a few words. While we were there, we cut logs, made repairs and generally helped out around the farm. On New Year's Eve, we had a party. I had located some brandy, Greet cooked a supper and the nine of us, plus a couple of neighbours and cousins, sat down and enjoyed the bringing in of the New Year. We didn't talk about the end of the war but we all knew it was coming. The weather remained dreadful with snow and freezing temperatures but at least we knew the Germans couldn't counter-attack in these conditions. During these weeks, the rest of the supply chain caught up with us, which was a great relief.

Although we enjoyed our time there, command was not pleased. This lull in the fighting had given the Germans time to re-group and re-organise. There was nothing we could do about it but at least we had time to train some of the new recruits who had just arrived. Thankfully, none of our unit had been sent home, we were still a motivated and organized little tank crew, heavily reliant on one another.

We were ordered to move out on the 13th of January. It was quite an emotional time, especially for Esme, who could not bear to let Billy go. He never told me but I think Billy asked Captain Haimes if there was any way he could stay but that would have counted as desertion. I can understand that he wouldn't want to go; he probably wondered what difference he could make to the war effort. He probably wondered if he would ever see Esme again, just as I wondered if I would ever see Evie. We all knew that things were getting increasingly dangerous as the Germans became more desperate.

Our first role was to support infantry, clearing the German army from the west bank of the River Roer. This was really difficult, nothing came easy now and after a few days fighting we came up against some German paratroopers who were well organized and extremely motivated and caused a lot of casualties. In the end, we had to use flame throwers and take the village one house at a time, the Germans just wouldn't budge.

Every mile we advanced was hard fought. The Germans would re-group and counter-attack, defending their homeland, whilst our raw recruits with little battle experience wouldn't press on, making it much harder. When we took the village of Dieteren in freezing fog, as soon as the engineers came in to build a bridge, the Germans were back with a machine gun team and so it went on.

The weather started to warm up a little which meant everything turned to mud, making it very difficult to advance. This was bad news for us in our tanks as the Germans were pretty fleet of foot, either with their 88mm guns or their *Panzerfaust*, which they just held on their shoulders and fired at tanks. All the time we knew we had the superiority in numbers and equipment as well as total dominance of the skies and it was only a matter of time but every one of us knew we could be killed, so we wanted to take less and less risks."

CHAPTER 15

Crossing The Rhine

"By the end of January, all the objectives had been met and our armies were all gathering ready to cross the Rhine. The German High Command must have known the size of our army preparing to cross into Germany, they must have known the game was up, but they had to keep fighting because they knew they couldn't agree peace with the Russians. The Allies were insisting on unconditional surrender which was impossible as long as Hitler was still alive.

Our next mission was Operation Plunder. We did wonder who came up with some of these names. We were to cross The Rhine at Wesel, behind the assault forces. Of course all of the bridges had been blown so the engineers had to throw Bailey bridges across the river. Our final objective, was Hamburg but it was still nearly two hundred miles away. The Allies had spent the last two months preparing the build-up for this great assault but of course the Germans had been doing the same on the other side of the Rhine. Intelligence told us that they had diverted many troops and equipment to the Eastern front where the Russians had been advancing, regardless of the weather. It later turned out that they had been committing dreadful atrocities against the German people, so it was understandable that the Germans were moving their troops around.

During this lull in the fighting, I was being asked to translate more and more. By now, there was a whole infrastructure set up to gather information about German atrocities during the war. Rarely did a day pass when I was not picked up and driven off somewhere to translate some harrowing tales from the local people. My Dutch steadily improved as I spoke more and I was interviewing a lot of German prisoners at the same time.

Operation Plunder began on the night of 23rd of March. On the 27th March 1945, we led the Division across the Rhine and into Germany. This is what all those years of fighting had come to. Despite the hardships and the horrors we were seeing every day, it felt good to know we were finally in the heartland of Germany but the war was still far from over and becoming seemingly more dangerous every day.

As we crossed over, there were broken gliders from the airborne assault everywhere. We had lost so many men in the attempt to capture the bridges to try and shorten the war, this really spurred us on. The next day we moved out and began to clear resistance in the woods. We had experienced the 88mm gun and Tiger tank fighting our way through Normandy which had been the greatest danger to ourselves once the Luftwaffe was overcome. Fighting our way through Holland it had been minefields which were incredibly effective and destructive but now in the 'Fatherland' itself, it was the cheap *Panzerfaust* that caused the most problems."

"What was this *Panzerfaust* you keep mentioning, Pepe?" asked Claudia.

"Do I? I didn't mean to, I hope it isn't an old man repeating himself. This was a long tube that one man could put on his soldier and fire a little bomb but they were incredibly effective and could knock out a tank. They were so fast to set up, it was difficult to defend against and, as we later found out, could be used by anyone, which made it all the more dangerous," replied Pepe.

"What do you mean used by anyone? You were just fighting the German army weren't you, it was the soldiers using these?" asked Claudia.

"You have to realize that the Germans were desperate by now. We were invading their homeland. The German army was calling on everyone to fight so not just the strong, young men but now they were asking for old men and children. I will tell you something about this shortly. They also had many different nationalities in their Army made up from people they had conquered over the last few years, who were themselves fanatical Nazis, this was another problem, that many of the people we were now fighting were fanatics. Yes, plenty of them just surrendered if they thought they were far enough away from their own officers but there were some who would rather die than give up.

Most people think that we were just fighting the Germans but the war was more than that. Yes, we were fighting plenty of Germans who wanted to defend their homeland but we were also fighting people from many different countries who had been taken over by the ideology of racial supremacy. I don't think that has ever gone away in parts of Europe, even today. It could happen again," said Leon.

"Surely not," said Roger. "Europe has been at peace for more than sixty years, you don't think we could realistically ever have war again in Europe? We all know each other, people travel, have holidays, do business, it seems unlikely."

"I know, it does seem unlikely," replied Leon. "But I still think it is possible. Those racial prejudices never go away, they just simmer. The Second World War showed how the entire world can be mobilized to do terrible things, it could happen again. I appreciate that you think these are the thoughts of an old man and not worth listening to but I saw at first hand over thirty years how things can change and what one human being can do to another, I hope that I am completely wrong, but more importantly that none of you ever experience war, it is destructive and ultimately pointless but that is the nature of human beings.

Anyway, back at the front, progress was slow with poor tracks through thick woods containing German paratroops, armed with the lethal *Panzerfausts*. The Germans were also very good with their machine guns. All the villages were filled with rubble, as everywhere had been bombed to prepare for our advance. There were refugees everywhere.

There was fighting every day now as the Germans defended every piece of land. We came up against anti-tank guns at Weseke and 88mm guns at the next village of Sudlohn. These were just sleepy German towns with only a few inhabitants but they were being fiercely defended. After every battle, our engineers came through with bulldozers to fill all the craters so we could move vehicles on, there was such destruction. Just imagine the same thing happening here, all the houses in this street being blown up, the road full of craters, people leaving with only a few possessions, no food and nowhere to go, it was awful. So much has been written about the war, the battles, the military successes, but so little about the plight of the people caught up in this. We wanted to hate all the Germans for the war and all the misery they had caused but it was difficult to hate the women and their children who were just trying to flee to safety, having lost everything. I tried to help where I could by speaking to them but we were in the heat of battle and trying to move forwards.

The next town was Stadtlohn. It had been completely devastated by RAF bombing; it was hard to imagine that anyone could have survived that barrage but the Germans took up very good positions there, made up from troops that had retreated from Holland. Every house had to be cleared individually. Fortunately, we were not too involved in any of this very dangerous fighting. Three hundred German dead were counted in the ruins of this little town, it was madness.

And on we went to more German towns and villages. We were now advancing by night as well as day, trying to catch the Germans during their retreats, not giving them the chance to regroup, it was hard and tiring but our commanders had learnt how adept the Germans were at re-grouping and counter-attacking and the damage they would cause, so it was better just to keep going and not give them the chance to do this.

Even though we were advancing so fast and had all the superiority, on the first of April, 'C' Squadron of our 11th Hussars were attacked while having their breakfast. About one hundred fifty Germans attacked, meaning that they had to leave their entire cooking kit behind. When we heard about it, we thought it was an April fool's but it was true. It wasn't long before we retook it and got all their cooking equipment back but it was very embarrassing for them and we didn't let them forget it!

We had made great advances into Germany covering over a hundred miles in a week against tough resistance. We were pressing forwards in lots of areas. We even came across a reformed 6th Airborne division who regrouped after the costly Rhine landings. Imagine our surprise when we saw some of them driving a steamroller! Everyone was commandeering whatever mode of transport they could in this rush forwards.

Unfortunately German resistance was getting fiercer and their battle tactics ever more professional despite their reduced capacity. We now came up against some canals where all the bridges had been blown and the Germans were massed on the other side. This was a natural area of defence and really the last obstacle between us and Hamburg. Beyond the canal was a wooded area on an escarpment about twenty-five miles long and a mile wide. What we then found out was that this was being defended by the Hitler Youth and their highly skilled instructors."

"What do you mean by the Hitler Youth? How young were they?" asked Claudia.

"Hitler's regime was one of the first to use propaganda. This had started way back when Hitler took power. He had some very clever people working with him, a man called Joseph Goebbels, who understood the power of radio which had only just become commonplace. The Nazis arranged for the manufacture of very cheap radios so that everyone could afford one so any young German living in the 1930s or 40s heard Nazi controlled propaganda every single day. The Nazis also controlled the press and the cinema, so it wasn't surprising that these young Germans all in their teens were fanatics because that is all they knew. There was no opposition to the Nazi doctrine so nothing was ever questioned.

They had been brainwashed with national and Aryan pride, patriotism and a hatred of the Jews. I know it is hard to understand, we have the freedom of the press, the BBC and everyone is entitled to an opinion. These young people never knew anything other than what they had been told by the Nazis. The British Government were able to transmit into Germany, from London, their own radio programmes trying to tell the Germans what was really happening in the war but the Nazis made it a treasonable offence to even listen to overseas broadcasts. In the first year of the war alone, 1,500 Germans were imprisoned for listening to London based broadcasts.

So, Claudia, we were fighting Germans as young as thirteen or fourteen, who were the most fanatical, armed with lethal weapons but hadn't even started shaving," replied Leon.

"Did you get to see any of these young Germans, the Hitler Youth?" asked Susan.

"Sadly, my lovely Susan, I did," replied Leon.

CHAPTER 16

The Ghost of Arminius

"This area we were now trying to take was called the *Teutoburger Wald*. It transpired that in 9AD, three Roman Legions of 20,000 men were ambushed and massacred by Germanic Tribesmen led by a nobleman called Arminius. As a result Germania never became part of the Roman Empire. One of the chaps in our division was a history teacher back in England and told us this story. It had been used as part of the Nazi's propaganda so the Hitler Youth had grown up with this; it was all part of the 'blood and soil' that the Nazi Party used to excite young Germans with.

We found out that the Germans regarded this as their last ditch stand and wanted to give a bloody nose to two of Britain's finest armoured divisions. It clearly had tremendous propaganda value so the order to defend at all costs had probably come from the very top. Originally, there were only two companies defending this area but they were being reinforced and by the 2nd of April this had risen to seven. They worked in small groups, high on the ridge, and kept moving, very mobile making it difficult to take them out with artillery. Many of them were good shots and they specialised in sniping at officers and tank commanders. We suffered a lot of casualties as the battle started. The Germans were in a great position and had all the latest weapons, do you remember I said that the German war machine kept producing weapons right up until the end of the war?" said Leon.

"But you were now so close to the heart of Germany," said Roger. "Surely you were capturing all the factories?"

"Yes Roger, you are right, we were now entering the heart of Germany but the Allies weren't surrounding the whole of Germany, this was one particular thrust, the Germans were still held out in northern Holland, the north of Germany, Denmark, lots of places, they even tried to retake Budapest in Hungary around this time, the fighting was going on all over Europe. In some cases, German armies were completely surrounded but didn't surrender, they were just boxed in until the end of the war, it was the same with the manufacturing, although the factories were being bombed all the time by the RAF.

So, the young Germans had all the latest weapons and experienced commanding officers as well as an excellent observation platform with the wood providing good concealment. What followed was a harrowing battle over three days. We would attack, get cut off, be rescued, and so it went on. Despite being heavily shelled the fanatical cadets kept fighting. Our tanks were brought up with flame throwers attached. I wasn't in one of those tanks but was a little way behind on one particular engagement. It was in the early evening and the sun was setting. I could see out of my driver's slit, which I had made as small as possible, as I said before, because so many drivers were being targeted by snipers, the tanks blowing out the flames with a deafening roar.

The trees and bushes would be engulfed and then we would hear the screams and see the cadets rise up on fire in the last frantic throes of life. It was the most terrifying thing I had ever seen. As the gunfire stopped, we left our tank and went up to the ridge where the Germans had been caught in the flames. There were fifteen or so charred bodies, distorted, some burnt beyond recognition, others still recognisable. I could hear Charlie Brooker sobbing behind me. He was stood over the bodies of two young men, no, not young men, children, barely thirteen years old, holding rifles, their faces contorted in anguish. Despite their horrific burns, we could see that their uniforms were too big for them, just children, nothing more than that." Leon put his face in his hands and started to weep.

"Pepe!" Donna and Susan both got up and went to their grandfather, hugging him as he started to shake.

"Pepe, are you alright?" asked Donna, but the old man couldn't reply as he gasped for breath in between his tears, gulping and shaking almost uncontrollably. The room was quiet apart from the gentle sobbing as everyone came to terms with what Leon had been saying, with the exception of Roger, who remained quiet. Leon's story had been harrowing and he had painted an almost unimaginable picture but it was the shock of seeing him so affected that triggered this collective grieving. In all his years as head of the family he had never once shown this kind of emotion, years of bottling up those memories were now pouring out.

"I think we all need some more tea," said Anthony, wiping the tears from his eyes as he got up.

Jonathan immediately rose and joined him. "I'll give you a hand, Dad," he said with trembling voice.

After a few minutes, Leon started to calm down and wiped his eyes with his handkerchief. Claudia was still sobbing but Jane was comforting her. The tea arrived, which everybody needed. Normal conversation resumed and the lounge was a buzz with chit chat. The *stollen* and mince pies were passed round and the mood lightened.

"Are you ok to carry on, Pepe?" asked Donna.

"I am alright, it just brought it all back, talking about it and being here with my beloved grandchildren, it was all too much. I am so sorry to have told you these things, perhaps there are some things that should remain unspoken," replied Leon.

"No Pepe, I want to hear everything that happened; your story is just amazing," said Benjamin.

"Only if you want to, Pepe," said Susan, her sisters nodded in agreement.

"I am alright to continue if you can all bear the ramblings of an old man but I must warn you all that I said this was the most terrifying thing I had seen up till then, in my whole life, but I was about to see something much worse. Do you think you can bear to hear about it? I can stop now; there are reasons why I have never talked about any of this," said Leon.

"You go on if you want to, Pepe," said Jonathan. "If anyone doesn't want to hear about it, they can go in the other room."

"Why are you looking at me when you say that?" said Claudia. "I saw you crying as well."

"Alright, I will continue. The battle for that ridge raged on for three days, none of the Germans would give up, as I said, they were fanatical, indoctrinated by the Nazi propaganda machine almost from the day they were born. The battle continued down into the local town and in some factories. They just wouldn't give up and many of those young, brave German boys died in the blazing ruins, burnt to death. These battles were almost Wagnerian, it was as though they were pre-ordained, the whole Arminius fight to the death thing, everything was burning, lighting up the night sky like a scene from hell. It must have served the German propaganda machine very well.

We had taken so many losses that by the 4th of April we were ordered to disengage and bypass the opposition, it was taking too much time and too many casualties to flush the last of them out, so we just moved on leaving the last cadets to be overcome by our infantry. These young cadets had seen off two armoured divisions. Much has been written about the fanaticism of the Japanese fighting to the last man to defend some God forsaken Pacific island, I can tell you that these young German lads were just as determined.

As I said, this was to be a last stand, so once we had bypassed them, we had a clear run of fifty miles or more completely untroubled. Some of the bridges were still intact; our engineers threw pontoons across the rivers where the bridges had been destroyed. Having reconnoitred an airfield and spotted four 88mm guns, we asked our infantry to take them out rather than risk losing more tanks in an open assault. They started to advance only to report back to us with some mirth that the guns were in fact dummies, but we weren't to know that. Even though we had overwhelming air superiority, the next day the Luftwaffe strafed and bombed our headquarters.

Onwards we went, another river with all the bridges blown, the engineers would arrive, erect another pontoon and so we crossed. I can't remember what we thought about all the bridges being blown up. The war was going to end soon and Germany would have no bridges. How were they going to be able to move about? Looking back it seems crazy; it didn't buy them much time. I doubt if we even thought about that at the time, all we wanted to do was get to Berlin and get home. I hadn't seen Evie for eleven months. I thought I might have got some leave in January but it didn't happen. We still wrote almost every day but I was desperate to see my new wife.

On 7th April, we the 8th Hussars took over the lead of the Division, capturing Emtinghausen. We tried to rush the bridge, which was defended by six self-propelled guns, but it was blown up. The plan of advance was now reviewed, as it was clear that each river crossing was heavily defended and all the bridges were being blown up systematically by the retreating Germans.

A couple of days later a German hospital was captured in the pine woods with two hundred patients. The Germans counter-attacked. During the fighting all the staff and patients vanished, we had no idea where they went to. The next day, our troops took a small town which had a huge store of gin. Soon afterwards German tanks were reported supported by infantry who were clearly trying to get their gin back. For the Germans there really wasn't much else to fight for, the war was lost. They were probably glad to be fighting us rather than the Russians anyway.

The next couple of days we advanced, crossing the

River Weser but then met German Marines which meant another prolonged battle. More men were lost; we just wanted to get the whole thing over with. We moved on and probed, taking Bremen, but it was firmly mined and heavily defended and the town was full of Panzers and divisions made up from the *SS*, so we just bypassed it, found a place to rest and re-organised, waiting for the final push to Hamburg.

On the 15th April, having rested and re-organised, the Division was soon on the move again. We moved towards Bergen-Belsen where we heard there was a prisoner of war camp," said Leon.

"You were at Bergen-Belsen!" exclaimed Roger. "That can't be possible."

"Why can't it be possible, Roger?" asked Leon.

"It was one of the most dreadful places from the war, like Auschwitz, what were you doing there?" Roger asked.

"I don't know why you are so surprised. We were the advancing troops through Germany. We were on our next push to Hamburg and we had to pass through this area. This is what happened," said Leon.

Roger looked utterly incredulous.

"What exactly is your problem, Roger?" asked Anthony.

"Oh come on, D-Day landings, V1 rockets, Bergen-Belsen, I mean. Heh, I am not disputing that Leon was in the army heading across Europe but De Gaulle, George Formby, it all sounds too incredible. I just think he is maybe getting a little confused," said Roger.

"Roger, how can you say that? Stop being so horrible," said Donna, clearly very upset.

"Donna, my sweet, please, it is alright," said Leon.

"What is this all about?" asked Claudia. "I have never heard of Bergen-Belsen, what do you all mean?"

"Claudia, I want you to be prepared for what I am about to tell you. You must stop me if it is too distressing," said Leon.

CHAPTER 17

Bergen Belsen

"We had just liberated a prisoner of war camp at Fallingbostel tucked away in the woods. There were more than twelve thousand prisoners. In amongst them were men captured at Villers-Bocage in 1944, where we had fought the previous year.

As we pressed on, we were told about a camp a few miles down the road. I was not in the front of the advance party but a number of vehicles behind. A message had come through that a Colonel Schmidt of the German Army had come to our HQ with a white flag, where he met our Brigadier Chief of Staff. He told the brigadier that our column was approaching a camp called Bergen-Belsen which contained civilian political prisoners and that Typhus had broken out. He had been sent by his General to propose that the area around the camp should not be fought over, in case the inmates escaped and spread the disease to both armies.

We were shocked to find the concentration camp. We had heard of these places. Auschwitz had been liberated by the Russians and it had been heavily reported. We had seen the photo of a warehouse with 800,000 pairs of shoes in but nothing could prepare us for this. It was agreed that as soon as our front line reached a certain point that the units of Germans should march out, but that the *SS* guards should stay behind to hand the camp over to us. It was then agreed that the guards should be allowed to leave and re-join the German forces.

It was a Lt-Col Taylor who had entered the truce zone to take charge of the Belsen camp. I was then called up to help translate. There were about thirty SS guards, all armed, surprisingly some of them were women and they were led by a man called Captain Joseph Kramer. Kramer held some papers in his hand that he wanted the Lt-Col to sign. Before we were able to look at them, there were gunshots from the camp. Kramer explained that there was some rioting happening in the camp as prisoners were trying to raid the food stores and that guards were opening fire. It was incredible that even though it was all over, the guards still felt they could kill whoever they wanted without fear; such was the loathing with which they regarded their inmates.

Lt-Col Taylor asked me to translate to the SS guards to lay down their weapons. Many of them were Hungarian but they all spoke German. At that point, I then joined Lt-Col Taylor and a Lt Sington in a tracked vehicle with a loudspeaker and we entered the camp. We toured the camp, making announcements in German, Russian, French and Dutch, telling everyone that the British army had arrived to take over the camp and that the prisoners should stay where they were.

This place was worse than you could imagine hell to be. I was completely numbed. Everywhere there were bodies but you could not tell which was which. There were open mass graves and corpses just lying where they had fallen and taken their final breath. The barely living were lying on the dead, gasping for life, whilst moving around aimlessly were the emaciated shells of what were once people with families, jobs and lives, reduced to skin and bone with no hope, tranced, existing somewhere between our world and death, oblivious to the suffering and sights around them. Here we were to free them from their subjugation but they had almost passed over to the next world. Mothers were clinging on to babies who had been dead in their arms for days, men, who a year earlier had been strong, skilled and useful, shuffled like skeletons, their striped uniforms hanging from their shapeless bodies and the smell of death hung everywhere.

We had no warning of what we were about to see, even if we had, we could not have truly imagined it; this was an abomination, something that should never have happened. The sheer horror was indescribable. It was more than the shock of seeing the inmates and their putrid existence, it was the understanding of the horrors that our fellow man could stoop to. The SS guards were all fat and healthy. There was clearly no shortage of food, these prisoners had been systematically starved to death and treated so abominably. It questioned everything we had come to know about our fellow man. Having just experienced how the Nazi propaganda machine had indoctrinated the young to fight to the death, we were now realising how monstrous that apparatus really was. These were not human beings but monsters not worthy to walk the same land as us.

Lt-Col Taylor immediately ordered all the SS to be arrested and put under guard as much for their own safety, I think. Once the troops saw what had happened here, the guards would have been in terrible danger. We now understood why the Germans were pulling troops away from the west to fight the Russians. The Russians had liberated Auschwitz at the end of January and, after that, showed no mercy to any Germans, man, woman or child. I started to wonder if I could ever look at any German in the same way again, could I show pity or forgiveness?

I left the camp and returned to my crew, where I was immediately drilled about what I had seen. I couldn't tell anyone, in fact, I shut down completely and was left to my own thoughts. I think the others knew not to press me on this, they all found out for themselves in the next few days.

An operation began to try and save as many of the prisoners as possible," said Leon.

"What do you mean to try and save as many as possible, the allies were there with food and medicine, why wasn't everyone saved?" asked Benjamin.

"These poor souls were so emaciated there was hardly anything left of them. The first food given to them, standard army rations, made them even more ill, many died when their stomachs bloated, also the water supply was contaminated, so everyone was dehydrated. The British forces who were left to sort out the camp did an amazing job converting a local Panzer barracks into a hospital, finding German civilian nurses to help, but it all took time. It took almost a month just to process all the prisoners and move them out of the camp. As soon as the last prisoner left, the camp was razed to the ground with flame throwers. It was a very dangerous job for those left behind because of the typhus and other diseases. The numbers were quite staggering; when we arrived there were 60,000 prisoners. Did you know that Anne

Frank was in Belsen?" asked Leon.

"Anne Frank of the diaries?" asked Paul.

"Yes, that's right," said Leon. "I didn't know this at the time, only when I read the diary, I found out that she and her sister were at Belsen, she died only a few days before we freed them. If only we had arrived earlier, we could have saved many more. I am sure if we had all known about the terrible things going on in these camps, we would have pressed on during January and February regardless of the weather. Many soldiers became wracked with guilt, even though it was the Germans and not us who had done these things. There were many reprisals that broke military codes against the Germans but they were not reported, so many people were seeking vengeance.

You know I said that the water supply was contaminated, that was a parting gift from the German soldiers. Even though their war was over, they still felt the need to persecute the Jews. It wasn't just the allied soldiers who wanted revenge, the prisoners turned on their former captives at one of the satellite camps and killed about a hundred and seventy of their former guards. Who could blame them?

Even after liberation, 14,000 prisoners died, such was the level of privation they had endured. In the end, the troops trying to help the former prisoners fed them on a kind of gruel, which was known as 'The Bengal Famine' mixture, a mix of rice and sugar which was pretty disgusting but was easier to digest. I am told it had to be mixed with a little paprika to make it even vaguely palatable. Although so many subsequently died, many were saved and went on to have full lives.

The British Army did everything they could to try and save as many as they could, it was impossible to imagine how ordinary Germans could have agreed to this, then, just as we tried to rationalize it, we heard that thirteen days after we entered Belsen, the Luftwaffe bombed one of the hospitals in the Displaced Persons camp, killing several patients and a Red Cross worker, it was only a few days before the end of the war but showed the spite and hatred the Nazis had for the Jews," said Leon.

There was silence in the lounge in Finchley. Here they were, some sixty years after the war had ended, but Leon had momentarily taken them all there to that hell, there were no tears, just complete shock. Leon had been their father and grandfather; he had lived a very ordinary life bringing up a close knit family. He went to work every day, they went to the park and had holidays, he would carve the chicken on a Sunday and would always toast *L'Chaim*. He had never spoken of the war and none of his family had ever known what he had seen. It was hard to imagine that a human being could have absorbed all of this, keeping it so close and never talking about it. Susan wondered if he had ever spoken about it to Evie, she had certainly never heard her mother mention anything.

Tears were falling once again down Leon's face, which he mopped away. In turn, everyone had tears, but rather than the uncontrollable sobbing of earlier, the family was calm. Donna took Leon's right hand. He didn't look up but offered his left hand, which was taken by Claudia and so on until the whole family was connected in one circle. They sat motionless and silent, even Roger knew that this was a time to say nothing. After a few minutes, Leon lifted his head and gave a deep sigh. It was as though he had released himself, that a weight had been lifted. Perhaps he had spoken about it before, to people like Billy Jackson, his lifelong friend who had been with him during the war, who may have understood better than most but to finally tell his family was a relief. It wasn't a burden lifted, Leon had never regarded it as a burden, over the years he had come to terms with what he had seen, he hadn't felt it was something he could describe for many years as it remained so raw but it was a relief that he was now able to talk about it. He felt it was important for the family to know, after all, they were half Jewish and this was their history.

"I am sorry everyone, I know that was quite shocking. You may know a little about the concentration camps from programs on the television but nothing could really convey the horrors we saw. Even now I don't have the words to really paint an accurate picture and for that I am glad.

Despite the horrors that we had seen the war was still going on and we had a job to do. We pushed on towards the town of Soltau which was found to be heavily defended by infantry and 88mm guns, so we surrounded it. The town was then bombed by our artillery and attacked with all the latest flame throwers. We found that the Germans were defending every last building and the easiest way to flush them out was with fire, rather than putting too many of our troops at risk. We just got used to seeing men burnt alive. I don't know what was worse, knowing that these ordinary German soldiers were dying the most horrible death or the recognition that we were now completely sanitized to it. I think that perhaps after Bergen Belsen and all the other stories we were hearing of other concentration camps being relieved, our attitude towards the Germans changed. Many of the troops no longer saw them as human beings but categorized them all as monsters. It was understandable; we were seeing things that were completely unimaginable at home, the sheer brutality and depravation.

Soltau fell by nightfall and we moved on to Harburg, a suburb of Hamburg our ultimate goal. The plan was to capture as many bridges as possible and then cut off the autobahn to cut off the German 1st Parachute army," said Leon.

"What do you mean cut off the autobahn?" asked Jonathan. "This was during the war, surely the Germans didn't have autobahns then?" he said.

"Germany was one of the most advanced countries in the world under Hitler. When he took power, he initiated huge infrastructure projects, including the building of the autobahns or motorways. The Germans had their first motorway almost thirty years before we did in England. We all remember the Nazis from the war and the terrible things they did, but the Germans were highly educated and had the most advanced economy in Europe, like they are today.

On the 19th of April, our tanks were advancing near Hamburg. As we turned onto the autobahn, German 88mm guns opened up on us. Our Commander, Wingate Charlton, ordered hulls down, which basically meant getting in the tanks and closing all the doors. He was in the lead and started to return fire, knocking out two of the guns. At the very next village, Charlton went forwards to reconnoiter, or take a look in layman's terms, spotted four more 88mm guns and then just overran the position, knocking them all out and taking a load of prisoners. He got a DSC for that. I must admit that we were all quite surprised to see the way he went a bit gung-ho, but I think he just got too close and rattled the Germans, who looked like they surrendered pretty quickly. Anyway, he was rewarded, I suppose that's what happens if you went to Eton, the rest of us following him didn't get a mention but we were all there, although he did mention me a bit later.

The next couple of days were quite strange, the forests were teeming with Germans with their *Panzerfaust* and 88mm guns but we just bypassed them and headed up the autobahn. Of course, these roads weren't designed for the weight of tanks and tracks and our air-force had been bombing them previously to disrupt German troop movements. Up until then, the German army had been moving mostly by train but by now we had destroyed so many of their tracks, they were using the roads more.

We pushed on to the River Elbe and took the town there. While we were waiting for orders we spent the time shooting at German ships on the river and trains going by on the far banks. It was like being at the fairground. We felt as though the war was coming to an end but of course we were just a microcosm of what was going on all over Europe. Our positivity was severely dented a few days later, when an *SS* regiment and Hitler Youth, along with assorted sailors and policemen, counter-attacked. The battle went on all day. When it was over there were more than sixty dead. This was on the 27th of April, so near to the end of the war. You could say they died for nothing.

The Germans were just not giving up and we found ourselves fighting all sorts of people who had made their way back to the fatherland to defend it., sailors, policemen even submarine crews. They had plenty of 88mm guns now not needed by the air defence of Hamburg as our own air force could hardly bomb the city with us in it."

CHAPTER 18

The death of Hitler and the end of the war

"We were now shelling Hamburg itself and on the 29th of April, a delegation came to discuss the surrender of the city. I was involved in the translations with various German Officers and the negotiations went on for some time, but eventually on the 1st May, General Woltz arrived with a white flag. It was quite strange to see a German general arriving in a car carrying a white flag after all the fighting that had been going on it seemed an anti-climax. The reason it had taken some time to agree the surrender was that the order had to have come from Admiral Doenitz. It coincided with the announcement of the death of Hitler in Berlin and Doenitz assuming responsibilities. I was there at the surrender as translator. Even though they were defeated, I couldn't help but admire how smart General Woltz looked as he surrendered. The German uniforms were impressive but clearly he was a broken man. That same afternoon, we entered the ruined city.

What we saw was shocking. The city had taken such a pounding two years previously and had never really recovered. The bombing of Hamburg was said to have been greater than the atomic bomb on Nagasaki in Japan. 40,000 people died during the bombings in 1943, in a firestorm that just made people spontaneously combust. Can you imagine it being so hot that people just burst into flames? We didn't see that, of course, but we did see the city in ruins. As our tanks rolled into the streets, women seemed to crawl out from the rubble with babies and small children desperate for food. The stench was unbearable with bodies rotting under the debris. We had been fighting our way through the countryside, where the Germans had access to basic foods, often growing their own, here in the cities, transport and infrastructure had broken down or was directed at the army defending Germany, the citizens had been left to starve. For many of the allied soldiers, this was a very difficult time. Seeing these desperate women naturally made us all feel guilty and want to help but we had just seen what the Germans had done to prisoners at Bergen-Belsen. The women in the streets of Hamburg were wretched, they had nothing but they were nothing like as thin as the prisoners we had seen a few days earlier," said Leon.

"What did you do, Pepe?" asked Claudia.

"I didn't do anything, Claudia, and I am ashamed to say it. I think I was filled with hatred, I just tried to block it out, there wasn't much we could do anyway, we were the spearhead of the advance and had to keep moving but I remember ignoring them as they wept and begged. It is not something I am proud of but by then we had seen so many terrible things, this was just another one; that is what war does to you," said Leon.

The old man took another sip from his water.

"Can I get you some more, Pepe?" asked Susan

"Actually, I would like a small brandy, please," he replied. This was most unusual for Leon, who rarely drank, other than the family toast but nobody was surprised. He was pouring out something he had bottled up within him for so many years. Everyone could see the strain on his face, a small brandy was no less than he deserved.

Taking a sip, Leon made himself comfortable in his chair and continued his story.

"On the night of the 4th of May, the news came of the surrender of German forces in Germany, Holland, Denmark and Norway and that hostilities were to cease at eight the next morning. After the surrender of Hamburg, we were ordered to move onto Kiel, which we were glad to do because of the stench in Hamburg. It was in Kiel when Victory in Europe was declared on the 8th of May 1945. The feeling when victory was declared was incredible. My first thoughts were that I would be home in a few weeks, with Evie in my arms, I had a vision of a warm beer in a country pub, a clean bed, a job, a house, all those normal things but I couldn't have been more wrong. There was so much to do and my languages meant that I was to be kept very busy."

"What do you mean, Leon? Surely the war was over, what else could you do?" Roger asked provocatively.

"Roger, please, call me Pepe, it is the name I like my family to use and you are my family, you have been a good husband to Donna, I love you like a son, as did Evie," he replied.

Roger blushed and nodded but could hardly look Leon in the eye, he felt ashamed, he didn't really know why he was questioning him, he had never had any time for Leon or the rest of the family, he had spent his life working and trying to get on, but maybe he had missed out on something; seeing the family all together as one, the children sat around their grandfather, something that would never happen to him, he felt overcome by emotion. Suddenly, feeling heavy and lost, he slumped in his chair, welling up, tears forming at the corner of his eyes. Donna put her hand in his; he took a deep breath and tried to compose himself.

Leon continued. "Yes, you would think that the war was over and we could all go back to normal but what did it really mean? Germany, like much of Europe, was crushed, destroyed. There was little infrastructure. We had been bombing all the railways, roads, factories, for months, years in fact, since 1940. The crops hadn't been looked after this year as the allies advanced, there were terrible food shortages, a lack of medicine, no fuel, no government, no law and order," said Pepe.

"What happened to all the German soldiers when they surrendered?" asked Benjamin, who was on the edge of his seat and hanging on every word.

"The day that Germany surrendered, the guards and the prisoners swapped over. I know it sounds crazy but that is more or less what happened. It wasn't the case everywhere, during our advances, we were taking hundreds of thousands of German prisoners, there were 250,000 after the Ardennes offensive, 325,000 after the Ruhr. When Germany surrendered there were already three and a half million German soldiers in the custody of the Western Allies and who knows how many being held by the Russians. The plan had been to ship them all back to England until after the war and look after them there but as more and more were captured or surrendered it became clear that this was not an option. The logistics of getting them there was impossible, let alone housing them and feeding them at a time when Britain was still being rationed. At the same time, the Germans still held many thousands of allies in captivity as well as all the political prisoners and Jews in various camps. In these camps, the guards became the inmates and vice versa," said Leon.

"Did they just hand over their guns and swap places then?" asked Benjamin, his voice rose with excitement.

"It was something like that but of course in many cases it didn't end well. As our troops and the Americans and the French advanced, we found these prisons and generally took a formal surrender from the German officers. We couldn't just let everyone go, they had to be fed and looked after, so in many cases they just swapped roles. Some of the prisoners had been held for years and had been treated badly by their guards, others were just filled with hatred and wanted revenge. Nobody knows how many guards, Germans, Austrians, Hungarians, so many different nationalities who helped the Nazis, were beaten and murdered those next few days. We heard stories of Germans being beaten to death by clubs and thrown out of windows, there was so much hatred. The Allied soldiers didn't stop any of it, it was difficult to; it might have ended in riots or more unnecessary killing, anyway in many instances we felt that it was well deserved. I know this is such a terrible thing to say now, we are living in a country where everyone has rights, where there is law and order but that was a different time, a different place. Many of the prisoners had seen their entire families wiped out, often by the *Kapos*, some by gas, torture, starvation or by the guards with a single bullet to the back of the head. How do you begin to rationalize with someone when they have been through that? This was the start of the period of healing and it was not pretty."

"Did you see some of this happening, Pepe?" asked Paul.

"I am sorry to say that I did. I was travelling everywhere, acting as translator, trying to identify the perpetrators of war crimes as well as helping to organise prisoners. There were people everywhere in such a state, one moment euphoric because the war had ended and then crying, distraught at the realisation of it all.

Although the German Army had surrendered, as you can imagine there were still a lot of weapons available to everyone. This made the art of retribution easier but equally there was the risk of die hard Nazis still fighting. In theory, all of the German prisoners were meant to be under the auspices of the Geneva Convention but the allies were worried that the Germans might mount some kind of guerilla campaign against the occupation. Because they belonged to a state that no longer existed they were re-named 'disarmed enemy forces' and basically had no rights," said Pepe.

"But surely that made the Americans worse than the Nazis?" said Benjamin.

"Perhaps," replied Pepe. "But from the time we landed in June the previous year, Goebbels was inciting all Germans, the army and the ordinary citizens to fight to the last man, he wanted to create something called 'The Werewolves' to fight a long resistance campaign. You have to remember that once we were in Europe, we were able to listen to all the propaganda, we genuinely felt that there were German terrorist cells everywhere. This is partly why so many of the German Army were incarcerated in the *Rheinwiesenlager* camps, where they could be kept an eye on, well away from trouble. There were so many of them, far too many for us to look after so we transferred control of these huge camps to the Germans themselves! Even the guards were former German soldiers and they were armed," said Leon.

"That's incredible," said Jonathan. "Giving guns to the enemy you just defeated, weren't you worried they would turn the guns on you?"

"Not really, where could they go? Germany was defeated, we were all around them, we just didn't want to have our troops guarding millions of Germans, anyway, at this time the most important thing was food and cigarettes and these guards got extra of both for doing this work. They were still armed in June the following year," said Pepe.

"The following year! What were they still doing there a year later?" asked Jonathan incredulously.

"Dear boy, just think about the pure logistics of finding a home for that many people. Everything had been destroyed, there was no food in the shops; it took a very long time to sort out this mess. There were some Displaced Persons still living in camps five years later!" replied Leon.

"What are Displaced Persons?" asked Claudia.

"I will come to that, one thing at a time." Leon took another small sip of his brandy and passed his glass to Susan, who put it on the table for him.

"Something smells good in kitchen," said Leon. "I love the smell of Christmas food, it just reminds me of family and being together."

"The food can wait," said Paul. "I am going to turn it down, you have to finish your story, Pepe, we are all on tenterhooks."

"Could you bring me a couple of Florentines please, I didn't realize what hungry work this storytelling would be," said Leon.

"Yes, please Dad, me too," said Benjamin.

"And me!" said Hannah and Olivia simultaneously.

"I will make up a plate of *yummishes* to keep us going," said Susan.

"I'll help," said Jane.

"Me too," said Donna.

The three sisters went through to the kitchen and looked at each other for a moment, in a state of shock.

"Did Pepe ever mention any of this to either of you before?" asked Donna.

"No, not once," they both replied.

"It just seems so extraordinary, the things he went through and saw. He has always been such a gentle man but saw such terrible things. Roger has been really shaken, I have never seen him like this before," said Donna.

"I think it has been good for him, and definitely the grandchildren, well all of us really, come on let's make up a plate to keep us all going and get back to it, it is the most extraordinary thing I have ever heard, let's get back before he nods off!" said Jane.

They all giggled and proceeded to make up some blinis with smoked salmon and crème fraiche, some prawns in croustade and cream cheese and strips of salt beef on crackers, a very traditional plate of what Evie always called *yummishes*. This was a staple of the Aleksandrov household and although everyone squealed with delight when the huge salver appeared in the middle of them, no-one was surprised by what they saw. This plate had appeared and been devoured every Christmas for as long as they could all remember. Jane offered it up to Leon first, who took the smallest of the salt beef. He smelt it and waited just a moment, savouring all the memories that a familiar smell conjures. The previous couple of hours had already brought back so many memories, some which had been buried for seventy years, and with good reason. This was one memory that could linger.

The salver was quickly devoured, with only a few pieces remaining, which Benjamin and Jonathan saw as an opportunity and shared the spoils between them. Glasses were topped up and they were ready to listen again. There was a hush as everyone looked to Pepe, expectant and excited.

Pepe shuffled in his chair, lifted himself up slightly, and then craned forwards as if to address everyone.

"Where are my Florentines?" he asked.

Everyone burst out laughing. Claudia ran off to the kitchen and brought back a plate of Florentines that were always in ready supply at this time of year. Leon tucked in, enjoying every mouthful. Within a few minutes, he was ready to continue.

CHAPTER 19

Displaced Persons

"Displaced Persons, I think you asked about, Claudia. During the war, the Germans, or perhaps I should say the Nazis, or was there any difference? Well, they imprisoned so many people, enemy soldiers, anyone who didn't agree with their ideology or quite frankly anyone they didn't like, particularly us Jews. As the allies advanced, Hitler didn't want there to be any traces of the terrible things that the Nazis had done, especially the concentration and extermination camps. From the summer of 1944, camps were emptied out and their inmates were shipped back closer to Germany. The first camp to be found was as early as July 1944, the month after we landed in Normandy, but it was discovered by the Russians. They told the allies what they found but nobody believed a word the Russians said, so it wasn't until January that we actually found out what was happening in these camps.

The Germans, by now, were in retreat, trying to defend everywhere, France, Italy, all along the Russian front. There were very few spare trains and trucks to transport the prisoners, so they were marched out of the camps and marched towards Germany, weak, starving people often without shoes or proper clothes, just walking along the roads and fields. So many died along these marches and their bodies buried in ditches or just left to be eaten by animals, so many bodies were never recovered and often not recorded. The Nazis were probably happy enough for people to die on the marches, they were having problems finding enough Nazis to do the killing of innocent people; this made it easier. Unbelievably, many of the people survived and made it back to camps in Germany, it is incredible how strong the human spirit can be, after all that time in work camps and the terrible marches, many of which were during that awful winter of 1944, and yet they survived.

These poor unfortunates made it to Germany and found themselves in some of the worst of the camps and yet they survived. At the end of the war, there were all of these people miles from home. For many of them, there was no longer a home, destroyed during the war, their families all annihilated. They had nowhere to go. They were given the name of 'displaced persons' or DP," said Leon.

"How many were there, you said there were already three and a half million German soldiers in captivity when the war ended, were there as many of these displaced persons?" asked Paul earnestly.

"Nobody knows for sure, as you can imagine, record keeping had lapsed towards the end of the war but there were probably between fifteen and twenty million people at the end of the war a long way from home and that was just in the western part, nobody has any idea how many there were now trapped behind the Russian lines. Probably not as many because all of the Germans, Austrians, anyone who might fall into the hands of the Russians were trying to flee to the west," said Leon.

"Why were they running away from the Russians?"

asked Benjamin. "Surely the war for them was going to be over whichever side they surrendered to?"

CHAPTER 20

Retribution

"My children, this is something that is so hard to talk about. The war had been raging for six years. It would be lovely to think that at the end everyone would want peace but there was so much bad blood. It wasn't the same for everyone you have to understand. The English and American armies hadn't had Germans on their soil. England was bombed, and for that they hated the Germans, especially their terror weapons like the doodlebugs and the V2 rockets, but that wasn't the same as having Germans taking over and the *Gestapo* living on your doorstep. It was only in the last months of the war, when the allied armies starting approaching Germany from the west, did we find out about the atrocities that were taking place and that is when our attitude towards the Germans started to change, but it was completely different on the Eastern Front," said Leon.

"Pepe, what was the *Gestapo*?" asked Claudia.

"They were the secret police that Nazis used to control populations. This wasn't a police force like we have here in England. They worked with the *SS*, most of them were fanatical Nazis. The *Gestapo* was feared because it stood above the law. If the *Gestapo* knocked at your door, you knew there was no-one you could appeal to, they were the law of the land and were only answerable to the highest echelons of the Nazi party.

They operated in every country that the Germans either invaded or annexed. They were at their worst in Russia. Hitler broke the original treaty he had with Stalin and ordered the invasion of Russia in the summer of 1942. The German army was incredibly successful initially and captured huge amounts of Russia before it all went wrong.

The reasons for the invasion were plain for all to see, Hitler had written about all of his ideas in *Mein Kampf* and it wasn't good news for the Russians or Slavs, as they were known. As the German Army advanced, the *SS* followed and arrested, deported, murdered, anyone they felt weren't sufficiently Aryan or even mentioned in Hitler's book. It boiled down to just about everyone unless they chose to side with the Germans. What the Nazis did there was terrible, exterminating whole villages, burning people alive, raping, killing, it must have been awful, but it got worse. When the war in Russia turned and the German army had to retreat, they were ordered to destroy everything on their way. Russia was laid waste and of course the pursuing Russian army saw all of this. The Russian women were raped and murdered; anyone who could work was deported back to Germany for forced labour.

This of course meant that the advancing Russian army saw what the Germans had done and it wouldn't be very long until they themselves were in Germany. As soon as they were on German soil, they sought retribution. Word quickly spread that German women were being raped and German men murdered, whether they were in the army or not. It was the start of a huge migration towards the west, where the Germans thought they might be treated better by the

English and the Americans. On the whole, this was true, which is partly why we had so many prisoners on our side at the end of the war. For many Germans, this was the first they had really seen of the war apart from aircraft flying overhead. Although Germany was very industrialized, a lot of it was still countryside and farming. Germans living in cities had had a difficult time, but the people in the countryside had been spared until the Russians advanced. The stories were terrible. The German people were now reaping the whirlwind they had started; nuns in particular were targeted as were the well off."

There was silence around the old man as everyone digested what he had just revealed. Like most people, their knowledge of the war was from history books and the sanitized versions that are taught in schools. This reality was difficult to comprehend, especially as the whole family, at one time or another, had been to Germany on holiday or business. Hannah and Jonathan had both been to Cologne on school trips and knew about the bombing of the city by the allies but it had all seemed so matter of fact and impersonal.

"Did you see any of this happening, Pepe," asked Anthony.

"I didn't see any of the rapes myself but I spoke to lots of victims of rape after the event but, worse still, I saw the bodies of women who had committed suicide afterwards. Many had survived the bombings but couldn't cope with the shame of the rapes," said Leon.

"But I thought you said this was the Russians doing it, you were on the western front?" asked Anthony.

"The Russians were terrible, they had an unofficial directive from Stalin that it was almost every soldier's duty to rape, but it also happened on the western side, I am ashamed to say. There was little law at this time and some soldiers took advantage of the situation. There wasn't the gang rape that occurred by the Russians but they took place all the same. This became part of my role at the end of the war, to translate and try and find out who the perpetrators were, but if I am honest, the officers didn't really want to bring any of their soldiers to boot for what they had done, everything was still too raw, many of the soldiers had been discovering German atrocities, as I said, this was only the start of the healing process," said Leon.

"What happened to you on the day of the surrender, when the war was declared over, Pepe?" asked Anthony, who had barely spoken the whole while Leon was telling his story.

"These were very strange times. Up until the final day of the war, we had been soldiers fighting a retreating army. We had a common enemy and a job to do, for which we had been trained. The day the war finished, our roles changed and we weren't really prepared. Of course, there had been planning from those above us but trying to enact it when everything had collapsed was difficult. You have to remember that there was no currency in Germany. Germany was no longer a state. Some of the original German hierarchy, like Admiral Doenitz, who had actually conducted the surrender, tried to form a German Government to get things running again but he and many others were arrested within a few weeks for war crimes. It would have been impossible to keep the people who had been involved in the atrocities that were coming to light in positions of power. You also have to remember that because of the total power of the Nazis, the *Gestapo* and the *SS*, there was no opposition party. Opposition in Germany meant certain death so, by association, all Germans had collaborated, an argument that carried on for years afterwards.

There were so many day to day things to sort out, the most pressing of which was how to feed everyone.

Our Division stayed in the Hamburg area, sorting out prisoners, helping to clear up the mess in the city and dealing with the tens of thousands of displaced persons, now roaming the ruins of Germany. I was kept so busy!

The war was officially declared over on the 8th of May, although incredibly one Germany army kept fighting for another four days but they were nowhere near us.

Fortunately, Uncle Isaak and I were now a permanent unit thanks to our languages and were stationed at Kaaks, north of Hamburg. Here we formed a small unit with the agreement of my squadron leader to specifically weed out any German officers or men who either served in *SS* units or had any connections with Nazi organizations or had served in concentration camps. Isaak and I, having the advantage of being multi-lingual and having already done some of this work during the advance to Hamburg, were able to gather a lot of information from the many displaced persons such as the Poles, Russians, Ukrainians, French and others who had been brought by the Germans from the occupied countries to work in Germany as slave labourers. Here we started to receive some of the 300,000 German troops from Norway and others from Denmark disarming them and moving them on to prisoner of war cages.

The displaced persons were aware that some of the returning Germans were trying to fade back into the local population and take up their former occupations. This was a time when identity papers had been lost in the last few months of the war, when it seemed that most of Europe was on the road, fleeing the fighting, so at times it was very difficult to prove who was who. A previous *SS* officer in his black uniform with skull and crossbones with peaked cap could look very different with a beard, dressed in rags, especially if they took on a limp and a lisp. However, we found that people were very forthcoming having suffered terribly and there was a general mood of retribution, which brought its own problems, as there were many personal scores to be settled. The displaced persons often knew those that had served as guards or commandants in concentration camps or were members of the dreaded *Waffen-SS*.

The DPs, sorry, Displaced Persons came to us willingly and pointed out certain individuals whom we visited and thoroughly investigated to establish their wartime activities, those whom we found out to have belonged to any of the organizations involved in war crimes were re-arrested and sent to special centres for further investigation and later prosecution.

In order to give Isaak and myself more authority and freedom of movement, and the ability to exploit our contacts with the foreign labourers and the local population, we were both appointed as Regimental Policemen. I expect you might be surprised to find out that your grandfather was once a policeman! A jailbird and now a policeman!" laughed Leon.

"Amazing," screeched Jane, they all laughed.

Leon took another sip of his brandy and continued. They could all see he was relishing this part of his story.

"From Kaaks, we moved on to another town in that area called Elstorf where we had fought a battle just before the end of the war. By this time, very much more was known about the atrocities committed by the Nazis in various countries, particularly concentration camps like Bergen-Belsen, Auschwitz and others. Posters, newspaper articles and pictures became available depicting conditions and appalling events. We displayed, in the Town Hall, all such material and made the whole population attend, in order to make them see for themselves what, allegedly, they had never heard about nor believed that these events ever took place.

To this day I am not sure how I feel about the reactions I saw. The impression we got was that these ordinary people were shocked and dismayed by the images but it seems impossible to believe that the industrial scale of the slaughter could have gone unnoticed, I think people preferred to ignore it, ultimately convincing themselves it was never happening. They must have all seen their Jewish neighbours taken away, never to return, and their possessions and homes re-distributed to more suitable Germans. What did they think had happened to those Jews, like the Edelmans, but I also understand the terrible pressure the SS put on all Germans to toe the line.

Some of my fellow soldiers were being de-mobilised and sent home but there was still a huge military presence, just the scale of all the displaced people was staggering. Gradually, many were returning home (if they still had homes to go to). The French Government requested 1.7 million workers to help bring in their crops and dig coal, which started to reduce the numbers but there were still so many people. It was pretty crazy, I can tell you. One thing that upset people the most, apart from the lack of food and shelter, was that even though the war had ended, the DPs were still not being recognized as individuals.

During the war they were prisoners, numbers, waiting for the gas chambers or being worked to death, they felt as though they didn't exist, which is why the Jewish community, despite all the privations continued with our beliefs, Shabbat, weddings, bar mitzvahs, to retain identity. Everyone hoped that as soon as the war ended, they could become a person again, with a name and a purpose, but this wasn't the case. There were just too many people and for months, maybe years, they remained one of millions on a list. Sadly, for the Jews in particular, they had gone from being Hitler's problem to becoming the Allies' problem.

I heard some terrible stories when I interviewed people but we had to remain dispassionate, not everything we heard was true either, fortunately Isaak and I never had to make judgements, our job was to gather the information by talking to all the various people in their tongues. This also gave me a great opportunity to practice some languages I hadn't spoken very much. Isaak and I were actually in quite a privileged position, we had plenty of food and cigarettes to keep us going," said Leon.

"There you go, Dad, smoking again, I still can't believe it," said Susan.

"I know, as I said before, during the war we all smoked, it calmed the nerves when we were fighting and relieved the boredom when we weren't. Even your mother smoked, everyone did, but we both gave up pretty soon after the war, we wanted to save to buy a house. Anyway, cigarettes were the best currency; it allowed me to trade a little, to pick up a few luxuries, which helped those six weeks fly by."

CHAPTER 21

A new role for Leon

"Towards the end of June 1945, I was called out of bed in the middle of the night, ordered to report to the quarter master to be fitted with a new uniform and be ready to be taken to the Divisional Commander's caravan, Major General L.O. Lyne at six thirty a.m. There, I was briefly interviewed by the General's aide-de-camp, Captain Easton and then by the General himself, who wanted to ascertain that I was in fact able to speak Russian, French and German, as he had been charged to become the commander of the British troops in Berlin. I was seconded from the 8th Hussars to General Lyne's personal entourage.

On the 29th June, we flew in a Dakota aircraft to Berlin, the group consisting of the General, his second in command, Brigadier Spurling, his ADC, his Batman and myself. Thus, I was the first British Soldier to enter Berlin.

The plan was initially to fly to Berlin to meet General Lyne's opposite, commander of the Russian troops in Berlin, General Gorbatov, in order to discuss and negotiate the eventual routing to and entry into Berlin of representative units of the British Forces. My job was to interpret the discussions between the two commanders, but in the end it didn't happen.

It is worth remembering that Berlin was captured after very heavy fighting by the Russian Army, the city having surrendered to the Red Army on the 2nd of May. Hitler had committed suicide a few days before, on the 30th April. I had seen Hamburg at first hand and so witnessed the devastation of a directed bombing campaign but that was nothing compared to Berlin, which had in effect been totally destroyed from the air and the ground. Berlin was the last great defence of the Third Reich and almost every building had to be fought for. The British air force had bombed Berlin right up to the start of the Russian offensive on the 20th of April, when more than two million Russian soldiers fired almost two million shells in the last two weeks of the war with planes, tanks, and artillery smashing what was left of Berlin trying desperately to get to Hitler.

This is when some of the worst atrocities happened, especially the mass rape of the women. There was no escape, the options were to hide and hope, succumb to an officer and hope to become a temporary single concubine and avoid the violence or suicide. Age was no barrier, nor were looks. It was difficult for women to hide, as everyone had to forage for food and water. By the time I arrived in Berlin, the frenzy had passed; the Russian high command had started to instil some discipline into the Russian army."

"What do you mean 'become a temporary single concubine'?" asked Claudia. "What's a concubine? How did that save them?"

"I was hoping I could have just skirted over this but you are all too bright and inquisitive, which is one of the reasons I am so proud of you, my grandchildren. When the Russians advanced in Berlin, it wasn't like fighting in the countryside where the tanks would rush across open ground covering miles and miles. Fighting in Berlin was quite literally every building, one at a time. As the Russians advanced very slowly, they would break into an apartment. These were lots of groups of men and women, because the Russians allowed women into their army to fight, unlike the allies.

These small groups would usually be under the command of one officer. Some of these groups would find some women, pretty ones first, but otherwise any woman they could find and lock them up in the apartment. They would go off fighting for a few hours then come back and rape them, continuously for a week or more, eight, ten, twelve men at a time. As they advanced through Berlin they would all move out and find another apartment a few blocks closer to the fighting and leave the poor women behind. These women had lost all their dignity, many suffered terrible injuries, where initially they may have tried to fight off the soldiers, but also internal injuries from what was being doing to them. Many were driven insane by what had happened; most were infected with venereal disease or gonorrhoea. Many just threw themselves out the windows and killed themselves, unable to live with the shame. The Berlin women realised, especially if they were pretty, that they could offer themselves to an officer. He would keep them for himself and his troops knew they couldn't touch her. It was the better of two evils; they also knew there was a good chance they might be fed better. This was a time for survival; people did what they had to do."

The family thought they had heard the worst of the suffering during the war. This was a complete shock. Donna looked across at her niece, Hannah, and started to cry, it was more than she could bear. She leant into Roger, who was himself trembling. Everyone was silent with their own thoughts.

Leon knew it was time to push on with his story, these were things that nobody should ever have to see or experience, his family were just hearing about it through his ramblings, to have been there and experienced it first hand was another story, no wonder he had suppressed it all these years and like many others who returned from the war.

Leon edged forwards and continued. "We stayed less than a week, trying to get meetings with our Russian counterparts, which were difficult to organise. We thought that Stalin had told his staff not to meet with us at that point whilst they formulated their plans and determined their strength. Their army was re-grouping and re-arming, unsure as to what might happen next. Eventually, we managed to have a discussion and determine how British troops might enter Berlin. We returned from Berlin and on the 5th of July 1945, the logistics were ready for representative units of allied Forces to proceed by road to Berlin. The leading car, a Humber Staff car occupied by General Lyne, Captain East, the driver and myself, eventually reached the border between the British and Russian occupied Germany at a bridge over the River Oder. The Russian sentry told me that he had not been informed that columns of various troops were to be expected intending to cross the bridge into what later became East Germany. I had great difficulty persuading him that we were on

186

perfectly legitimate business and urged him to call the officer in charge of this crossing.

Finally, a captain arrived to explain to us that we were not supposed to cross over at this particular bridge and that we were expected at the Friendship Bridge at Magdeburg. There was nothing for us to do but to turn the column round and proceed to the new location. The Magdeburg Friendship bridge had been built by American Engineers because all the original German bridges had been destroyed by either the advancing allies or the retreating Germans. It's hard to believe that only a few weeks before, we were an advancing army pushing forwards where we could but now we were having to ask the Russians where we could go and get permission. German *Panzerfaust* couldn't stop us but protocol and a Russian captain could.

Towards the evening of that day, we reached Berlin and our first overnight stay was in the famous Olympic Stadium where, in 1936, the Olympic Games had taken place, and where Jesse Owens, the American black athlete, won three Gold medals, much to Hitler's disgust. I had attended these games at the age of nineteen, which would probably also have been to Hitler's disgust if he had known that Jews were there. I had a sense of *schadenfreude*, this was one of Hitler's crowning glories, designed to personify the perfect Aaryan and the Aaryan race, the Thousand Year Reich, but less than ten years later, we were staying there as unwelcome guests representing the armies that had smashed that dream to pieces."

CHAPTER 22

Villa Lemm and the division of Berlin

"The following day, we proceeded to the small town of Gatow, a few miles outside the centre of Berlin, and to a very beautifully situated house called Villa Lemm. Billeting officers were busily engaged in finding permanent billets for all of the troops, which meant commandeering some German homes. Gatow was a suburb in the west of Berlin, not far from the infamous Spandau prison where Rudolf Hess was held," said Leon.

"Who was Rudy Hass?" asked Olivia.

"Rudolf Hess!" said Leon. "He was Hitler's right hand man for many years and helped him write *Mein Kampf* whilst they were in prison together. He flew to Scotland in 1941 hoping to negotiate peace with England. He was the last State prisoner to be in the Tower of London, after the war he was tried at Nuremberg and ended up in Spandau."

"Did you meet him, Pepe?" asked Hannah.

"No, I didn't, and nor did I want to, there might have been questions asked as to why a Jewish refugee wanted to visit Hitler's right hand man!

We were very lucky with Villa Lemm, it was quite lovely and had escaped all damage during the war and still had quite well maintained gardens. It was surrounded by fields and had its own military airfield that we were able to use. The area was entirely within our British zone. Albert Einstein had stayed there in the 1930s.

General Lyne, Brigadier Sparling, Captain Easton, the General's driver, batman and myself now occupied this villa. I couldn't really believe my luck, the house was beautiful and, whilst I didn't have any of the best rooms, it was much more comfortable than a Cromwell tank, a tent or a barn that had been some of my various homes the previous year," said Leon.

"Didn't Uncle Isaak stay there as well?" asked Jane.

"Not at this time, he was billeted elsewhere, although he did join me there later on.

My job was to accompany the General to all of the meetings that required me to interpret the negotiations between the Russians and the British. My first major historic task was to interpret the handing over of the area, which was to become the British Sector of Berlin. The Ober Burgermeister, Herr Reuther, performed this function in German, which I then interpreted in Russian to General Gorbatov and in English to General Lyne. It was quite a lot of pressure to get it exactly right, as you can imagine, a misinterpretation at a time of high anxiety would not go down well.

After this ceremony, we were engaged in daily meetings, lunches and occasional dinners with our opposite numbers, formulating the structure and general procedures for governing the city of Berlin. It was fascinating work and a pleasure to be involved in something that appeared to be constructive after the previous twelve months of destruction. It was also a relief to be away from the despair, although I couldn't help thinking about it all the time. Even when we went out, we were protected from the austerity that was all around. Food and drink were a plenty to the victors and we were the top of that particular tree.

The first weeks were very hectic and it seemed to me that I was virtually on duty twenty-four hours every day. Eventually, the General became aware of this fact and suggested to me that we should find another person to assist me. I immediately suggested that my old mate and comrade in arms, still with the 8th Hussars, now stationed in Berlin, would be an excellent choice to give us the required assistance. It was at this point that Isaak joined me at the Villa Lemm.

Another task was for us to meet and receive a procession of important people from London, such as the Prime Minister, initially Mr Winston Churchill and after the General election on the 5th July 1945, Mr Atlee and many Ministers and Military VIPs," said Leon as a matter of fact.

"Did you meet Winston Churchill?" exclaimed Jane.

"Yes, I spent some time with him, he was visiting in the run up to the Potsdam Conference and then of course he was there for the first few days. He was actually accompanied by Clement Attlee, the Labour leader, as the British general election was happening the same time as the conference that was going to decide the future of Europe. Mr Churchill had wanted the election to be delayed until we had victory over Japan," said Leon.

"What was victory over Japan? I didn't know they were involved?" said Claudia, fascinated.

"This was a world war, Claudi, it really was fought

all over. Japan joined the war on the side of the Germans. Mr Churchill had been fighting a world war and didn't want an election until it was all over. Japan had mainly been fighting the British and Americans after Pearl Harbour and continued until the atomic bombs, the Japanese didn't surrender until August, but by then Winston Churchill and the Conservatives had lost the election by a landslide to Mr Attlee's Labour Government," replied Leon.

"But Churchill had only just won the war, why did he lose the election? I didn't know that," said Benjamin.

"Everyone was fed up with war. For the British civilian population, the war seemed almost over a while ago. When the last bomb was dropped in March, everyone's attention was turning to life after the war; people were fed up with rationing and a low standard of living. Mr Churchill was a great wartime leader but his focus had been on defeating Germany, not the future well-being of the British people, the Labour party talked about introducing the National Health Service and full employment. Labour put together some popular policies while Churchill was still focused on the war and the new world that would be carved out after it. His focus was too much on the bigger picture for people more concerned about their own welfare than that of others," replied Leon.

"Politicians weren't the only important people we met, and many of these people we took on sightseeing tours of Berlin. On one occasion, we conducted a tour with Field Marshall Montgomery, accompanied by our own General Lyne, and visited, amongst other sites, the partly damaged Hitler's Chancellery."

CHAPTER 23

At Hitler's desk in the Reich Chancellery

"I had already been to the Chancellery, in fact, I was the first Allied soldier to go in there with Isaak. Many of the buildings were guarded by Red Army soldiers but with my Russian language, powers of persuasion, some cigarettes and my British military passes, I was able to enter what was left of the Reich Chancellery. Do you know that Hitler ordered this to be built in under a year and it was! At today's cost, it would have been a billion dollars, and yet they finished it in a year, they say it was actually finished forty-eight hours early and all the craftsmen were invited in to inspect it and Hitler addressed them all, thanking them. I expect they knew the consequences if it wasn't finished on time. I saw it after it had been bombed and it was still impressive. There were a series of chambers where visiting dignitaries would have had to pass to get to meet Hitler. The doors were seventeen or eighteen feet high. One of the halls was four hundred and eighty feet long, twice as long as the Hall of Mirrors in Versailles, which apparently really pleased Hitler. At a room behind was Hitler's study, another enormous room with a vast marble desk at the end.

Isaak and I opened the drawers and found a great many original, interesting historic documents, many signed and annotated by Hitler himself. We 'acquired' sheaves of these papers for later examination. I sent a letter home to Evie on Hitler's notepaper; you can imagine her shock when she received it! I continued to send her letters on the paper but gave the rest to the Imperial War Museum. Just pass me my satchel, please Roger, it is by your chair," said Leon.

Roger leant down and passed the bag across to Leon, who rummaged around for a moment before producing a couple of pieces of blank paper with some printing. He passed them first to Roger. It was easy to tell that they were quite old but of very good quality. Roger took them and looked in disbelief. Both pieces had 'The Fuhrer' printed at the top, along with an eagle and swastika. One of them had a scrawled note with the initials AH.

"Just a couple of pieces I kept, do you like them, Roger?" asked Leon.

Roger was speechless. He was realizing that everything Leon had been saying was true. These were not copies as part of some prank, he could tell immediately that they were the real thing; they lacked the crispness of modern printing but exuded quality. Everyone had arms outstretched to see and were leaning forwards.

"Amazing, just amazing," said Paul.

"Right place, right time, I suppose," replied Leon, quite nonchalantly.

CHAPTER 24

The Potsdam Conference

"Over the next few weeks, we were very busy preparing and getting ready for the Potsdam Conference. I am sure some of you will have heard of this, it was the big meeting at the end of the war to divide up Europe. Of course this had been discussed as far back as 1942, but the Russians had given so much, and advanced so far, that actually the situation now was completely different. For one thing, due to the huge losses the Russians endured to defeat the Nazis, Stalin felt they deserved much more. This ultimately led to the cold war but nobody could see this coming, apart from Mr Churchill, who always seemed to see the bigger picture.

The Conference took place starting on the 15th of July in the old town of Potsdam, just outside Berlin. It was attended by Mr Churchill, initially, for Great Britain, President Truman for the United States, Joseph Stalin for Russia and President Charles de Gaulle for France, who were all to sign the Peace agreement with Germany and establish the final demarcation lines between the four occupying powers. It was held at Cecilienhof, the home of Crown Prince Wilhelm Hohenzollern

The following day, Winston Churchill lost the election to a Labour landslide victory losing two hundred and nineteen seats.

My General was not involved in the talks but he attended as an observer. The number of people who were accredited to be present from the British Military Command of Berlin was very small indeed. I was fortunate enough to be the only non-commissioned serviceman who had an official pass, which was issued by the Russian Authorities who were in charge of security hosting the Conference," said Leon.

"So you got to meet President Truman and Stalin?" asked Paul.

"Yes, briefly, I was introduced to them, it was a relatively small affair. I actually translated for General Zhukov, the Russian general, during part of the conference. One of the big confusions came about when President Truman was economical with the truth about the atomic bomb which was very tricky," said Leon.

"This is all crazy," said Jonathan. "I have been reading all about this time and you were actually there with all these world leaders, it's just insane! My grandpa is famous, wait until I tell my friends!"

"Listen Jonathan, I was just there doing my job, I didn't have any influence on the decisions, I was just translating but I did appreciate the importance of it all, the things they were talking about. Carving up Europe, the various sectors in Germany, the futures of millions of people, the power of the atomic bomb that was about to be unleashed, it was quite extraordinary to see the fate of so many being decided by a handful of people and of course everyone had their own agenda.

It was quite shocking to see what a small role Great Britain was playing in this, it was pretty clear that the main players were the Russians and the Americans, we even had to change our leader halfway through because of the elections, I think the other countries knew we were a spent force, we were completely bankrupt, but for the financial help of the Americans, but equally everyone respected Mr Churchill as the guy who stopped Hitler. Winston was very concerned about the huge numbers of Soviet troops in Europe and feared another war, he saw Stalin as very unreliable and there was little that the Soviets said at Potsdam to make him change his mind.

I think the Americans felt the same, which actually made it harder to just send all the troops home. It turned out that this was the start of the Cold war which carried on for another forty years, until the Berlin Wall came down. I don't think anyone at the time thought this would be the case, after all, the war had been terrible, with so many lives lost but it was the Russians who had suffered most and they weren't as keen to help rebuild Europe, they were much more interested in their own security to make sure war didn't come to Russia again, as opposed to helping rebuild Europe which of course they just saw as the renewing of the same old threat and it was understandable.

If you could just pass me my satchel again, please Roger, ah thank you, let me see where it is… here we are!" Leon held up a small piece of card and showed it to everyone.

"This was my security pass, issued to me by the Russians for the Conference, this one was for the 19th of July," said Leon.

"This is just amazing," said Jonathan again, quite

unbelieving that his mild, quiet grandfather could have been part of such a tumultuous event.

"I still can't believe it," he said.

"Nor can I," said Donna. "We know you never wanted to talk about the war, which we kind of understood, but this is really extraordinary, why wouldn't you have mentioned this? These were some of the most famous people of the twentieth century and you were there rubbing shoulders with them!"

"Looking back, I suppose it was something quite special, but at the time it was just my job. In the army, you do what you are told. I was told to go to the Conference and translate and that is what I did. I knew it was important but I really was only just doing my job.

Anyway, the conference carried on until the 2nd of August, when all the declarations were made but we all knew there were big disagreements between the Russians and everyone else, but they had the biggest army now so it was very difficult. I think Truman had come with ideas of peace in Europe but by the end he felt the same way as Mr Churchill did about Stalin, that he couldn't be trusted," said Leon.

"Pepe, why do you always call him Mr Churchill?" asked Hannah.

"Sweet Hannah, he was a great man, when things looked pretty grim for England, he was there encouraging everyone, I can't believe Attlee would have been able to do the same, as nice a man as he was, he didn't have those leadership qualities about him. Even though Mr Churchill was coming from a position of weakness at the Conference, you could tell how much the other leaders respected him, it wasn't the same with Attlee.

I despise the way the popular press now call our Prime Ministers by their last name with no title. To be Prime Minister is the highest honour in the land, he or she is the culmination of all of our votes in a democracy. That is what we fought for and I think they should be shown more respect as much for them as for us, the people. The Prime Minister is the pinnacle of all our struggles to maintain freedom and the ability to determine our own futures and we should never forget that. It has been a long time since the end of the Second World War, there have been many other wars since but none as encompassing and certainly none that have involved the whole country being mobilised together, let alone the whole of the world; we should respect and remember what we fought for and one of those things is to have our own elected Prime Minister and not some crazy person like Hitler, who took us all to the brink of destruction by forcing his way into power.

I am sorry, these are the rantings of an old man, I know the world is different today; you have all grown up knowing only peace. The wars you see on the news are far away and really have no impact on you, but don't think for one moment that wars are a thing of the past, do you? Germany was a very educated country with some of the world's greatest thinkers and yet it succumbed to a very small group with a crazy ideology.

The German people in 1933 weren't racists, they didn't want to exterminate a whole race of people, but a relatively small group of Nazis used propaganda and violence, they were the masters of exploitation and knew how to prey on people's fears. These things can happen, remember I was there throughout the changes, they start very small and then they build up. Because they are small, they are accepted until it is too late, you don't see it happening or at least you think you don't. You always think someone will come along and stop it. One day, Jews can't sit on a park bench, the next they are being gassed. That was the problem, everyone was waiting for someone else to come along and stop it instead of doing it themselves, that is why it is so important that you all use your votes when it comes to election time, keep the democracy flourishing and never let it go, it is more valuable than you think.

It isn't a guarantee but it is one of the most powerful things we all have. Germany lost that and we all know what happened. Some say that Hitler was swept to power by popularity but it was never the case. In the 1932 election, he only had thirty-seven percent of the vote, Hindenberg had fifty-three percent of the votes and was re-elected as President, but he was an old man who didn't want power, he was voted in to stop Hitler but he died two years later. Hitler just took over, abolished the office of President and created a new position of Fuhrer or Leader. He was able to use his strong arm followers to make this happen, you see, even in a democracy, these things can happen, so you young people must always be vigilant and not take anything for granted, promise me, please!" Leon was quite animated.

"Yes, Pepe, we all know the importance of our vote, you have drummed it into us forever. You actually took me to the polling station when I said I wasn't going to bother," said Anthony. "You watched me go into the booth and waited for me!"

"And me," said Donna.

"Me too," chipped in Jane.

"And what about these young people, will you all be voting at the next election? Hannah and Jonathan are both old enough, Olivia and Benjamin will be very soon, don't ever take for granted what you have been given," said Pepe, letting out a long sigh.

"Are you alright, Pepe?" asked Claudia, leaning forwards and taking his hand.

"Yes, Claudi, I am ok, it just pains me when I think of what happened and I wonder if it could have been avoided, if only someone, somewhere, had spoken out in the early days before it was too late, all those people who died during the war and for what? The millions more who died afterwards as well," said Leon.

CHAPTER 25

The systemic starvation of the German people

"What do you mean? The millions who died afterwards?" asked Roger, who was now feeling a little more composed.

"Just because the war ended, didn't mean the suffering and misery ended. There were many concentration camp survivors who were almost starved to death and just died through lack of understanding by those that found them; you couldn't just give those poor unfortunates ordinary food. Then there were the brutal retaliations in the first few months after the war, nobody knows how many people died then but the worst was the starvation of the German people," said Leon.

"What do you mean their starvation? It sounds as though you thought it was organized?" asked Roger.

"It was," said Leon.

"By whom?" asked Roger.

"The Americans, the French, the British and the Russians, although we aren't really certain what happened on the Russian side as communication became frayed quite quickly after Potsdam," said Leon.

"I don't understand," said Roger. "Surely once the war was over everyone returned home and things got started again?" he asked.

"I realise it is difficult to comprehend. Unless you

had seen it, it is impossible to imagine the destruction. I saw at first-hand how difficult it was to get things started again. There were all the German military in prison immediately after the war. There was no way to send them all home, the trains had been destroyed, roads ruined, apart from the fact that we were still trying to find all the Nazis for war crimes. There were so many people being held and they had to be fed. Do you remember I told you how we weren't really following the Geneva Convention? This was part of a policy that seemed to come from America. There was something called 'The Morgenthau Plan'. This was something dreamed up by a Jewish American called Henry Morgenthau. He advocated the systematic destruction of German industrial capacity which would have led to the starvation of the German people as they would not be able to afford to import grain.

By the autumn of 1945, industrial production was reduced to around twenty-five percent of pre-war levels, thus preventing the chance of buying food imports. Germany was banned from manufacturing all kinds of things, certainly all their heavy industry was completely stopped, which would have created jobs. Hitler had actually ordered that all German manufacturing should be destroyed as their armies retreated to ensure the end of the Third Reich and to make sure the allies didn't get it, but his Minister, Albert Speer, stopped all of these orders getting through.

He knew that Germany would need to be rebuilt and kept a lot of it intact but now the allies were doing their best to cripple Germany anyway. The allies slowed oil production to a trickle, closed down many factories, kept the labour force imprisoned; confiscated and destroyed factories, even fiddled the books so the Germans couldn't be credited with some of their exports. There was constant talk within our group about what was going on. The officers knew about it, they had briefing papers but we were seeing both sides. Every day we could see the Germans struggling for food, shelter, even the most basic existence but they were the ones who started the war. There was an attitude with many, especially anyone from the occupied countries, the French, the Dutch, in fact, especially the Dutch, who had such a terrible time at the end of the war, that the Germans were getting what they deserved.

Our office produced a report in September 1945, where we estimated that half the children in Berlin under the age of three would not survive another year. The infant mortality rate in Berlin at that time was nearly one hundred percent. This was such a difficult time for us. We were living in comparative luxury at the Villa Lemm, we had access to food and drink that had been seized from the German military at the end of the war, huge piles of wines, brandy and other luxuries, as they say 'to the victor, the spoils' but surely we were better than that? There was just this policy of stopping food getting to the Germans.

In our zone alone in Hamburg the following year, 100,000 Germans were in the last stages of starvation whilst the British Army had food piles that were rotting away. Of course word started to get out about all of this. People started to say that the Allies were as bad as the Nazis, starving people to death, Red Cross trains were being turned away and sent back to Switzerland, foreign governments were denied permission to send food to German civilians, permits were refused; someone somewhere was making life very difficult for the Germans. We of course were at the sharp end of things trying to organise everyone, to keep control, whilst starting to work things out with our Russian counterparts, who were suspicious of everything.

It is hard to believe but food parcels from Britain to Germany in 1945 were forbidden. This was all happening at the time of the Nuremberg trials, where famously Arthur Seyss-Inquart was hanged for withholding food from the Dutch, there were a lot of double standards at that time. The French were particularly harsh towards the Germans. Official rationing in the French Zone in January 1947, almost two years after the war, was down to four hundred and fifty calories a day. I never saw this, but apparently German churches were flying black flags to mark the deaths from starvation," said Leon.

"How do you know all this, Pepe?" asked Jonathan. "Why have we never read about this?"

"Roger asked me this earlier on, how I knew many of the statistics and what appeared to be sensitive information. You must understand that I was in the middle of all of this. The group of people I was working with were running things in Berlin and in the British occupied zone and, although I was only a minion following orders, we were such a small group that I heard so much directly or indirectly. I was privy to many of the conversations and I saw a lot of the paperwork. It was all brushed under the carpet.

At the time, emotions were running high, as I said, this was all leading up to the Nuremberg trials, the newspapers and radio were full of detailed accounts of Nazi atrocities. Nobody believed those things could have been done by a few people. The press were suggesting that all the German people were culpable, at that time there was no research done into the subjugation of the German people by the Nazis, we in the free west still believed that all of those German people had a real choice, it was only years afterwards as more and more was written about the 1930s and 40s that it became clear that the German people were either brainwashed or brutalized into submission and coercion. I think that debate still goes on today," said Leon.

"How did you feel, seeing all this going on, seeing the German people starving?" asked Roger, who seemed to be completely absorbed by everything that Leon was saying, as were the whole group who were all craning a little closer, hanging on to every word the old man uttered.

"I am not really sure. We were rushed off our feet, constantly firefighting, there was so much to do, an awful lot of it completely frivolous. I think I told you that we set up headquarters at a place called Villa Lemm. Isaak and I worked there together. We were in charge of the Military Guard and a large number of German civilian employees. It was many of these employees who used to tell us what was really going on. They had family and friends who either saw at first hand the problems or knew someone. Because we spoke German, and weren't really English, they felt they could talk to us.

Also whilst working there, we took frequent journeys to the *Kommandatura* to interpret discussions between the Russians and the British. We used to hear a lot of classified information during these talks.

It was during this time that I got to know General Gorbatov on the Russian side very well, he then became the Soviet Commander of Berlin. We heard things that seemed completely unacceptable but what could we do. There was no press and we would certainly have been drummed out of the army if we had said anything, this is why I always say to you not to believe everything you read in the papers, you will be amazed how very powerful people can have the news adapted to suit their own agenda. We knew this mass starvation was going on but hardly anybody did or has ever found out since.

All this time, from the 5th of July up to the 30th of August, I was always in the company of General Lyne, whom I had known for a while, as he had become the Commander of the 8th Army as we pushed through the Siegfried Line in our advance to Germany and Hamburg at the end of the war. He was the first military governor of the British Zone of Berlin. It was he who picked me to work for him and it was certainly much more interesting and better rewarded work than many of my old comrades in arms.

"Roger, sorry to trouble you again, my satchel, please. Thank you," said Leon.

As before, Leon looked into the weathered leather satchel and pulled out two more sheaths of paper.

"This is a letter from General Lyne about my work for him. Roger, why don't you read it out, please?" said Leon, passing the piece of paper to Roger.

His son-in-law cleared his throat and proceeded to read out the words. "'From the Headquarters of the British Troops in Berlin, August 1945. To Whom It May Concern. Corporal Aleksandrov has been employed by me for the last two months, whilst I have been commanding the British Troops in Berlin, as my principle interpreter. He speaks fluent Russian, Polish, German and French. He is not only a very fine linguist but has also a great deal of intelligence and common sense. His services have been quite invaluable to me when dealing with Marshall Zhukov and the senior Russian and French officers of the *Kommandatura*. Signed L O Lyne, Major-General Commander'. That is pretty impressive," said Roger, nodding.

"That is so cool: Zhukov!" said Benjamin.

"It was just my job, I didn't mean to show off, I just wanted you to see. If you look at the other piece of paper, Roger, you will see that it is from my old commanding officer in the 8th Hussars. Evie had been trying to contact me; the mail became very erratic with all of the sudden moving around. It was alright within the Regiment but when Isaak and I went to Berlin, we were out of the normal loop. Letters were crossing over and for a few weeks Evie didn't know where I was or even if I was still alive, she was very worried because she had heard how fierce the fighting was in the last few days of the war with only the fanatics left."

"Pepe, this letter says you were as good at political work as you were at fighting, what did he mean?" asked Benjamin.

"I presume you are interested in the fighting rather than the political work, Benjamin? We were the spearhead of the allies fighting the Germans, we had many battles, as you can imagine. After Holland, there were no more organized pitch battles against the German Army just many small skirmishes. I have told you a little about these, how our weapons changed. We came across more and more fanatics as we fought our way into Germany and then the cities, many of these were just children, the *Hitler Jugend*, who had been mercilessly indoctrinated by propaganda since the day they were born. These fanatics would fight to the death, which is why we developed flame throwers and other terrible weapons. We always had air superiority but that wasn't helpful in many instances so it had to be face to face sometimes," replied Leon.

"So, did you...?" Benjamin's voice trailed away. It was the question they all wanted to ask but nobody really wanted to hear the answer.

"Did I kill a man? Is that what you want to know? The simple answer is yes. I killed more than one. It is something I have had to live with all of these years and it was the same for all the men I fought with and for the Germans on the other side. Outside of the war, we were all ordinary men. I have worked at the engineering company in Finchley all my life, I am a family man, I was that man before the war and I wanted to be that man after the war. What happened in-between was a moment of madness by everyone.

Those poor German children with their *Panzerfaust* bigger than them, honestly believing they were doing the right thing because they had been told every day since they could understand that the German people were superior and to protect the Fatherland. It was madness but there was no choice. Goebbels had told the German people that they must fight to the very end, he called it Total War. This insane doctrine was policed by the *Waffen-SS*, Hitler's most fanatical people.

When we were advancing through Germany, we

found German soldiers, young and old, shot in the back by the *SS*, this is how they made them fight. Yes, I killed men, it is not something I am proud of, I think about it almost every day, it is not something that you can shut out, however much you try. At the time you are regarded as a hero, doing your job, but afterwards the guilt is terrible."

"I just find it amazing that you never spoke about it. You must have said something to Mummy?" asked Susan.

"No, sweet Susan, not even your mother. She knew not to ask and I never said anything. When I returned home, we just started our lives like any normal newly-weds except, of course, we had had a two year gap apart.

Back to my little story, otherwise we will be here until the new year! Because we were the centre of things - British in Berlin - we had a great many functions at Villa Lemm for visiting dignitaries. These were great fun to organize and the house was very well suited to having big parties with well attended gardens, a swimming pool, a boat house and access to a lovely lake where we were able to go swimming as well. You can imagine with the big parties, and all of the top brass visiting, we had plenty of fine food and wine, which made my situation quite difficult. I had seen how the Nazis had taken everything for themselves and left us Jews with nothing and now the conquering armies were doing the same.

Of course, I enjoyed the food, having been on rations and military food for the last year it was lovely to taste something wonderful but I felt very guilty, especially with all the stories my German workers were telling me. On one hand, I was in the British

Army; on the other hand, I felt I was one of them, an underdog all my life. I had wanted to fight, I wanted to fight for freedom, for me and my family but wasn't I fighting for freedom for everyone against these terrible people? But who were the terrible people? I had been on the move since I was a baby, long before Hitler ever came to power. There had been so many people trying to make my life difficult since the day I was born. Had I been fighting against all of them, had I now become one of them?" asked Leon.

"But you weren't hurting anybody, surely you were trying to help them, weren't you?" asked Donna.

"Do you remember what I said to you all, 'If only someone had spoken out'? Well I didn't, I just carried on doing my job like everyone else. We knew it was wrong that we had everything and the Germans had nothing, but we were the victors, they were the vanquished, maybe a sub species less than ourselves, this was the same thing that the Nazis said about the Jews, the Gypsies, the homosexuals, that misguided superiority. Who were we to say that we were superior to the Germans? The Bible taught us to forgive but it was difficult and, quite frankly, there wasn't much appetite for forgiveness in the summer of 1945.

We continued to hear reports of starvation amongst the German people and considered trying to get some food to them from Villa Lemm, but it would have been a grave offence. To this day, I am ashamed I didn't try. It took another year before food was allowed to be sent into Germany. In the meantime, a very large number of Germans died of starvation whilst many of the German Army who were being kept in camps with no shelter and inadequate clothing also suffered.

One of the arguments was that countries like Britain were still being rationed and people could barely feed themselves there so why should they pay to feed the Germans at their own discomfort? It was a perfectly valid argument, if not a very Christian one.

The persecution of the Germans was much worse in the east. Under the Potsdam agreement signed by Stalin, Churchill and Truman, all the Germans in Poland and Czechoslovakia were to be repatriated, a kind of ethnic cleansing. They were unceremoniously thrown out with nothing to their name, many died on their march to nowhere. Was it divine retribution for the expulsion of the concentration camps and the death marches of 1944 and 1945? Perhaps it was. We know that many died on these forced marches but no-one was interested, they were Germans and they deserved it. Anyone who tried to help by giving the German children food was shouted at by his fellow Czechs or Poles as a Nazi. At the Nuremberg trial, Adolf Eichmann was found guilty of ordering forced marches from the concentration camps back to Germany and was executed for it but after the war, when the same thing happened again, nobody was punished, the double standards were shocking.

Nobody knows for sure how many Germans died during these expulsions from the east, all of the numbers during this time were too big to record, it was just part of what was going on but it would have run into the millions. There have been no end of books written and films made of the Holocaust and the deaths caused by the Nazis but so little has been written about the fate that befell the Germans after the war, and bear in mind I am a Jew who had to leave and lost family during the war to the Nazis. Somehow the fate of the Germans has been swept under the carpet ever since, not just the Germans but anyone who sympathized with them. Whilst it is amazing that anyone ever forgave the Germans, it is also amazing that the Germans forgave anyone after what happened to them at the end of the war, perhaps it was just guilt on their part.

Do you know that the allies even banned the production and supply of fertilizer to Germany? The Germans had their land reduced at the end of the war and then there were all the millions of Germans expulsed from Poland, Sudetenland, Czechoslovakia and fleeing the Russians, and we, the allies, were actively stopping them feeding themselves. I remember one day we had a telegram arrive from some agency in Denmark saying they had thousands of tons of meat spare but we were forbidden from acquiring it for the Germans, there was food available in Europe but not for the Germans, we were starving them to death. It got so bad that in hospitals, the staff were deciding which babies not to feed to give the strongest ones a chance, there were even instances of cannibalism that we had to act to stamp out."

Leon sighed, dropped his head and seemed to slump in his chair as though the life force had been exhaled.

"Leon!" shouted Roger, rushing forwards to catch the old man as he fell forwards into his arms. Everyone was shocked and the group crowded together.

"I am alright," said Leon, quite frail. "It is the first time I have spoken about this since it happened, you would think after all of these years the pain would have subsided but it doesn't go away, it sits there all the time. I really am alright but Roger..." Leon paused.

"Yes?" asked Roger, still holding him.

"Please, call me Pepe."

They all burst out laughing, including Roger, who helped Leon upright. Everyone shuffled back into their places, taking the opportunity to have a sip of their drinks or nibble on some of the remaining *yummishes* and Florentines.

Everyone could see that Leon was exhausted emotionally. It was obvious, that with all the memories flooding back, how painful it was for him to be going back to that time. Whether he had thought about this before or blocked it out for all those years, nobody wanted to ask him. It would be awful to think that he was carrying this baggage around with him every day.

"We never heard about any of this," said Roger. "It doesn't seem possible that all this could go on and nobody knew."

"There was an information blackout," said Leon. "Germany had itself become the biggest prisoner of war or death camp in the world. The Germans were being herded together and systematically starved but, because this area was controlled by the militaries of the conquering nations, it was relatively easy to control the news reports, remember they had already opted out of the Geneva Convention, aid agencies weren't allowed in to help," said Leon.

"What changed, Pepe? How did Germany become the great country it is today? I mean, the Germans make everything and are very wealthy," asked Paul.

"It was probably just time but there were some

notable acts. At the end of the war, Truman had Herbert Hoover, a previous President, as his kind of food Tsar. He went all over the world, spotting where there were surpluses and where there was famine. He organized to move food around because Germany wasn't the only country starving. It had been a world war and many countries were now without food. In 1946, news was getting out of Germany about the terrible conditions the German people were enduring and American Senators became very vocal.

Truman asked Hoover to look at what could be done. He introduced something called 'the invisible guest'. He asked Americans and Canadians to lay a place at their table which represented a starving German child or mother. This brought the German plight into American homes and started the change in attitude. Once the barriers created by the allied victors were removed, Germans got on with re-building their farming economy and were soon able to feed themselves again. It is amazing how resourceful people can be when they have their backs to the wall. This was not the Allies' finest moment but eventually it passed." Leon went to take another sip of his brandy but his glass was empty. Pre-empting this, Benjamin leant forward with the bottle and topped him up.

"I don't think I have ever seen you have a second glass of anything," said Jane.

"This has been quite tiring for me; I think I deserve another drink, don't you? *L'Chaim!*" he said, raising his glass to everyone.

The others sought their own glasses, quickly topped them up, and, led by Jane, toasted.

"To Life."

"*Budmo*," shouted Pepe.

"Health and Happiness," they replied and everybody chinked glasses.

CHAPTER 26

The End of the War Parade 21ˢᵗ July 1945

As they took their seats again, Leon returned his glass to the little coffee table by his side and continued.

"On a lighter note, I haven't told you all about the big parade we had.

On the 21ˢᵗ July 1945, there was a very big military parade. Members of the Government and high ranking officers with equally high ranking guests from the other occupying powers, took their place on the saluting base to view the march past and drive past of all the British and Canadian forces stationed in Berlin, amongst them my own regiment, the 8ᵗʰ Hussars.

On that occasion, I was to be in charge of General Gorbatov, whom I accompanied to the saluting base, explaining to him the procedure and then followed the Prime Minister, who by now was Clement Attlee, and other dignitaries in an armoured half-track, inspecting the troops. Needless to say, my comrades in the 8ᵗʰ Hussars were quite impressed to see me inspecting them.

Ten thousand men representing Britain's fighting forces took part in this parade. It all started when our guns fired an eighteen gun salute in honour of Winston Churchill and to signal the start of 'The End of The War Parade'. The fact that the Desert Rats were given such a significant role in the parade was a fitting epitaph. There were men in that parade who had fought from the deserts of North Africa all the way into the heart of Nazi Germany.

During the past few weeks, the troops of the Division had been assembling in Berlin. The city was a scarred and blackened ruin, strewn with rubble, but flag-poles had been erected, stands built, vehicles painted and equipment polished for the big event. You could easily have thought that all the tanks and vehicles were new, they were so shiny. Firstly, we drove through with all the various units taking the inspection, the look on the faces of my pals as they saluted as I drove past in the vehicle behind Winston Churchill. That was a great moment, I can tell you! With the inspection over, the March Past began down the Charlottenburger Chausee.

Taking the salute was former Prime Minister Winston Churchill, Montgomery, Major General Lyne, and Clement Attlee, you can see them all there in this picture, along with other high ranking officers," said Leon, passing round a picture he pulled from his satchel, which was now by his side.

"Where are you, Pepe?" asked Claudia.

"I was at the front by the stand on the edge of the road when this was taken, fortunately just out of camera shot. Once all the units were past, the military bands led the marching contingent. This was a pretty unique spectacle and one I never forgot, in fact, we all talked about this day when we got together after the war.

Later that day, in the newly formed 'Winston Club', Winston Churchill met the men of the Division and spoke to the Desert Rats. I was there, not in my usual capacity, but as a member of the Division, it was great to be back with my old pals and off duty for a while.

After Berlin, the 8th Armoured Division was moved to the town of Itzehoe, in Schleswig Holstein, where it stayed for a year before moving to the Dutch border to help with internal security and occupation duties, I didn't go with them as I was working full time for General Lyne, so I stayed at the Villa Lemm, which was probably a lot more comfortable but I did miss my old friends.

I continued my work for General Lyne until the end of August 1945, when he was replaced by Major General Eric Nares.

During that time I had some leave, I was able to return to England on a couple of occasions to see Evie and make plans for the future. I stayed in Berlin up until the end and was eventually demobbed in January 1947," said Leon.

"What does demobbed mean?" asked Claudia.

"It was short for de-mobilised. It meant that my days in the army were over and I could become a civilian again and resume my normal life. In the eighteen months after the end of the war, over four million of us were demobbed from the services and sent back to England. We were given some cash and a new suit, shoes, shirt, tie and a hat, ready for civilian life," said Leon.

"What did you do for those eighteen months? I know you told us about the parade and being at Villa Lemm, but what else happened?" asked Jonathan.

Berlin was a complete mess. Our role was to get it functioning whilst managing the Russians. It was very busy and I also spent time translating, helping with the preparations for the Nuremberg trials of the Nazis. It was hard work but at times I felt we were making a difference, although it really was a time of two steps forwards and one step back. There was a constant stream of refugees and all the logistics that goes with it.

Berlin after the war was like nothing you can imagine today. This had been one of the most culturally advanced cities in the world prior to the war but now all the infrastructure was destroyed. Germany had lost so many men that the women were in the streets removing the rubble by hand with wheelbarrows. There was little running water and electricity. There was no currency as the Government had collapsed. No tobacco had been sold legally in Berlin since May 2nd and yet cigarettes became the stable currency. On the black market, a single cigarette cost from fifteen to twenty marks, a dollar and a half to two dollars, at the official rate of exchange, depending on its quality. American cigarettes were considered the best, and the standard black market price for a pack of twenty was three hundred marks, or thirty dollars. The value of a pack of Chesterfields ran as high as seventy-five to ninety dollars.

I'd conservatively estimate that at least two million of the three million Berliners left in the city, that had once been home for nearly four and a half million, were now engaged in butt collecting. The butt collecting in Berlin, I do not hesitate to say, was the most intensive on earth. Remain stationary on a Berlin street while you smoked a cigarette, and likely as not you would soon have around you a circle of children, able-bodied men, and whiskered old men, all waiting to dive for the butt when you throw it away. Because of our privileged positions, Isaak and I had access to a lot of American cigarettes, which were much easier to re-distribute to the poor Germans than trying to smuggle food out of Villa Lemm. It was said that some American soldiers made their fortunes during those crazy days just selling cigarettes.

CHAPTER 27

My War ends, my life begins

"As I said, I stayed in Berlin until the end of 1946 and was demobbed in January 1947 to resume normal civilian life. Evie who, in the meantime, was herself demobbed a very short time after the war had rented a room in Chiltern Gardens, Cricklewood NW2. We lived there until 1950, when we moved again to here and we had our three wonderful children and life settled down to some normality, and of course we were then blessed with our five wonderful grandchildren.

While we were in Berlin, Isaak and I were able to spend our free time together and we would talk about how life would be when we got home. We dreamed of sitting at home on a Sunday and having lunch with our families, the simple things."

"I can't believe that after everything you went through, and all the work you did, that you just came home, it just seems unlikely?" asked Roger.

"Roger, my boy, this may be difficult to understand. You are right; I was in an extraordinary privileged place during extraordinary times. I met the world's leaders, the conquerors and I was privy to some of the great discussions that mapped out the future of the world at the end of the war. I was offered a role to continue the work being done in Europe. We knew that there would have to be a military presence there for years to come as the Cold war was just shaping up. There were still hundreds of thousand, if not millions, of Displaced Persons. I was offered jobs with the British Army, the British Government and even with UNRRA, with whom we had been working," said Leon.

"What was UNRAA?" asked Claudia.

"I am sorry my precious, in those days all sorts of organizations were being created and they all had acronyms. UNRAA stood for United Nations Relief and Rehabilitation Administration, this was an American agency funded primarily by American money. I worked with them and they knew me and utilized my languages," said Leon.

"I still don't understand," said Roger. "This seems like an amazing opportunity, why didn't you take it?"

"Why did these people want me to work for them? Because I had all of my languages and I knew all of the people involved in the post war operations in Berlin on both sides. It was a great opportunity that's for sure but why was I there in Berlin?

My life had been a constant journey, I was a nomad, I had no place that I could call home, the Nazis had tried to exterminate all of my immediate family and my entire creed. I now had an opportunity to put down roots, to know that if I planted a garden, I would see it grow. The job offers were amazing, General Lyne also asked me to join his Chief of Staff back in London but I craved an ordinary life where I could determine my own future. I know you look at this house that Evie and I have always lived in and wondered why we didn't move somewhere bigger, you probably wonder why I remained happy at the company here in Finchley.

When you have seen how quickly and easily things can be taken, like the Edelmans, when you see a starving woman exchange a gold watch for half a loaf of bread, you realize that money means nothing. What the war taught me is that family and roots are what are important. For all of us to be here together, not just at Christmas but throughout the year, family, relying on one another, loving one another that is what is important to me and it was important to Evie too. All the money in the world couldn't have saved those poor souls who were persecuted. Instead of making money, they should have stood up and spoken, nothing has changed today. Now even more of the money is held by fewer and fewer who do not seem to want to help their fellow man, money really cannot bring you happiness.

I appreciate that you may not all agree with me, you have your lives, you have grown up in a world that seems to be very safe, you are not lying awake at night waiting for a jackboot to kick in the door and take everything that you have, but there is no guarantee that it will always be like that. I don't want to frighten you but we must not assume that things will always remain the same.

I visited Auschwitz many years ago with Isaak and one of the other visitors said that this is what happens when you let authority take over. The guide said that that although that was true what we must watch out for is when we are collectively compliant because that leads to collective culpability. Nazism arrived with a relatively small fanfare. They didn't start exterminating Jews on day one, it took many years of drip feeding the German people their hateful propaganda until eventually almost all Germans accepted what they were told, they became compliant, unable or afraid to contest what they were hearing. As time went on, they became culpable whether they were actually holding the gun to a head or moving into a flat previously owned by a lovely couple known as the Edelmans.

There will be another war, we are a destructive species; I just hope that none of you witness it. War brings out the worst in people. There were lots of stories of heroism, of course, but the majority of people just let it all happen around them. They were fearful and it was easier and safer to go along with everyone else instead of standing up, but where did it lead?

When the war ended, I knew that I wanted a quiet life, hopefully full of love and happiness and I promised myself that I would try and do the best I could to make all those around me safe, content and happy. I think I have done that quite well as I look at you all here.

After everything that happened and all that I had seen, I realized that life was for living, it is the moments we share that are important, not how we are dressed or the car that we drive."

Roger shuffled uneasily on his seat. He had never got to know Leon, not really, and had always been quite dismissive and he knew this upset Donna, who loved her father in a way that Roger had never been able to feel about his own parents. This day had been a revelation for him. As he sat in the middle of one of the closest families imaginable and had listened to quite the most extraordinary story, there seemed to be some clarity in what had been a very opaque existence. Now was not the time to say anything, he would confide in Donna later, but he was already telling himself that his life must change, that he had taken a wrong path somewhere along the way.

"Now my family, those smells tell me that a splendid Aleksandrov family dinner is on its way. Thank you all for being so patient with an old man. This was a story I thought I would never tell; it just seemed the right time. I hope I haven't upset you too much, I know that some of it was quite difficult but perhaps this has helped you understand who I am and who you are. In many ways, your lives have been influenced by what I saw. We never pushed any of you too hard, we always tried to give you room to express yourselves, all we wanted was for you to be happy, to have opportunities and to always know that your family were close by. Family is everything, if you know that you can go out into world with no fears, whatever happens to you, we are always there for you. Now let's eat!"

"Pepe, that was amazing, extraordinary." The whole family clamoured around Leon, kissing him, holding his hands, adjusting his rug for him; the room was alive with emotion, genuine heartfelt love for Leon and one another. Leon may have created the spark but this was a love that had been generated since the day they were born by Leon and Evie, who had created an unspoken pact to fill their family with love and belonging and they had succeeded.

As they drifted out to the kitchen and the dining table and started bringing through plates of meat and vegetables, Leon sat alone by the window. He was content. The bustle from the other end of the room and the familiar smells of an Aleksandrov family Christmas reminded him how lucky he had been. As for his story telling, it was a tale he thought he would never tell. As he closed his eyes, he realized it was the first time that he didn't momentarily see charred bodies and the horrors of those last months before the war's end that had plagued him for so many years. He knew that, at last, he could sleep and be at peace. This would be his longest and deepest sleep.

TIMELINE OF EVENTS

13th June 1917	Leonid Aleksandrov Born
1920	Left Russia during Russian revolution
1920	Escaped to Bessarabia
1921	Escaped to Warsaw
1922	Moved to Danzig
1925	Moved to Kracow
1928	Moved to Berlin
1933	Hitler Comes to Power
1935	School closed down by The Nazis, Leon started work aged 16
1937	Left Berlin for Lausanne in Switzerland
1938	Moved to Paris.
1939	Left Paris for Nevers (France)
1939 23rd May	Leon arrested
1939 24th May	Sentenced to two months in prison for being an illegal alien.
1939 5th July	Arrived in Finchley, England

1939 7th July	Started work at Gaumont Engineering
1939 1st September	Poland invaded by Germany. Britain declares war. Leon joins up at Finchley Recruiting Office in The Pioneer Corps
1940	Sent to Westward Ho! Devon
1940	Evacuation from Dunkirk. Churchill becomes Prime Minister. Battle of Britain
1940	Moved to long Eaton near Derby
1941	March, met Evelyn
1943	June Joined Royal Armoured Corps
1943	September 22nd married Evelyn
1943	Training in Farnborough and Aldershot
1943	Joined the Kings 8th Hussars , Armoured reconnaissance division for the 8th Army The Desert Rats
1943	Stationed at West Toft Norfolk
1944	Underwater training at Lowestoft in preparation for D-Day

1944 June	Moved to Gosport near Portsmouth
7th June	Landing at Arromanche as part of the D-Day landings
8th June	Captured Bayeaux
14th June	De Gaulle arrives at Bayeaux and declares The French Government
11th – 30th June	Battle of Villers-Bocage. The German Panzer Ace Michael Wittman knocks out 14 of out tanks in 15 minutes in his Tiger
July	Re-group and take the strategically important town of Caen
12th August	Battle of The Falaise Gap which captures most of the German 5th and 7th Panzer armies bringing the campaign in Normandy to an end
17th August	Capture of Livarch
21st August	Crossed River Toques
23rd August	Lisieux Taken
23rd August	Paris Liberated
28th August	Crossed the Seine at The Foret de Bretonne

3rd September	Discovery of V1 rocket site at Haebrouch
11th September	Crossed into Belgium. Battle of the Ghent Canal
23rd September	Entered Holland at Sint Oedenrode; Operation Market Garden
October	Battle of The Maas
10th November	Wessen Canal
7th December	Tudden
16th December	Battle of the Bulge commences
13th January 1945	Taking of St Odilenberg
16th January	Taking of Dieteren
23rd March	Operation Plunder
27th March	Crossing of The Rhine
7th April	Captures Emtinghausen
15th April	Enter Bergen Belsen
19th April	Approach to Hamburg
30th April	Hitler commits suicide
3rd May	Hamburg Surrenders

4th May	German forces surrender
8th May	War in Europe ends
29th June	Flies to Berlin with General Lyne
5th July	Leads British forces to meet Russian counterparts at Friendship Bridge, Magdeburg
6th July	Arrives at Villa Lemm
15th July - 2nd August	Potsdam Conference
21st July	Berlin Military Parade
30th August	General Lyne leaves
1st September	Major General Eric Nares takes over
January 1947	Leon Aleksandrov demobbed

THANK YOU!

To my Reader:

Many thanks for buying *World War II Survival*, I hope you enjoyed reading it and found it to be thought provoking.

If you did, please post a review at Goodreads or your favourite social network site and let your friends know about *World War II Survival*.

Grant

CONTACT DETAILS

Cover designed by: László Zakariás

Published by: Raven Crest Books
www.ravencrestbooks.com

Follow us on Twitter:
www.twitter.com/lyons_dave